Rogue Saints

Spirituality for Good-Hearted Heathens

D0010930

Jerry Herships

WESTMINSTER
JOHN KNOX PRESS
LOUISVILLE · KENTUCKY

© 2019 Jerry Herships

First edition
Published by Westminster John Knox Press
Louisville, Kentucky

19 20 21 22 23 24 25 26 27 28—10 9 8 7 6 5 4 3 2 1

Unless otherwise indicated, Scripture quotations are from the New Revised Standard Version of the Bible, copyright © 1989 by the Division of Christian Education of the National Council of the Churches of Christ in the U.S.A., and are used by permission.

Book design by Sharon Adams
Cover design by Allison Taylor

Library of Congress Cataloging-in-Publication Data

Names: Herships, Jerry, author.
Title: Rogue saints : spirituality for good-hearted heathens / Jerry Herships.
Description: Louisville, KY : Westminster John Knox Press, 2019. |
  Identifiers: LCCN 2018044503 (print) | LCCN 2019005556 (ebook) | ISBN
  9781611649352 (ebk.) | ISBN 9780664264420 (pbk. : alk. paper)
Subjects: LCSH: Non-church-affiliated people. | Good works (Theology) |
  Work—Moral and ethical aspects. | Church attendance. | Church membership.
Classification: LCC BV4921.3 (ebook) | LCC BV4921.3 .H47 2019 (print) | DDC
  248—dc23
LC record available at https://lccn.loc.gov/2018044503

Most Westminster John Knox Press books are available at special quantity discounts when purchased in bulk by corporations, organizations, and special-interest groups. For more information, please e-mail SpecialSales@wjkbooks.com.

Rogue Saints

To Laura and Hudson:

*My life would have been empty
and shallow without both of you in it.
You have brought joy to my life beyond
what I can measure or put into words.
I thank God every day for you.*

Contents

Acknowledgments

This book goes out to many tribes:

First, the bartenders and servers who I have come to know and love over my lifetime. You are some of the hardest-working people I know, and you do it with a smile on your face. Your hospitality is something the church could learn a lot from. I especially want to thank the bartenders and servers, past and present, of Don's Mixed Drinks, Euclid Hall, White Chocolate Grill, the Irish Rover, Parry's Pizza, and Interstate Kitchen & Bar. You've always made me feel welcome, and you're always glad to see me. You are either genuinely good people or outstanding actors. My money is on the former.

Second, the rebels, rogues, and misfit saints of After-Hours. Your willingness to be, try, and do something different always amazes me. You polka to your own accordion man, and I dig it! You are some of the most compassionate people I have ever known, and I am proud to be a part of your community.

Third, the homeless of Denver. You have taught me what grace, kindness, generosity, and love look like.

Despite horrible conditions in your life, you carry on. You smile in the face of adversity and laugh when you probably want to cry. Your lives are a lesson in resiliency. It is an honor to be with you.

And finally, Jessica Miller Kelley and all the people at Westminster John Knox for taking a chance on me TWICE. I can't tell you how much that means to me. Between the curse words and the drink recipes, you might have created a new sub-genre of religious publishing. Keep believing in people. . . . It will change the world.

Introduction: Happy Hour

Don't worry. I'm just as stunned as you are that you are reading my second book.

Last Call was the story of how I picked up the pieces of my dashed dreams and created a new normal (as a *pastor*, if you can believe that). But even though I'm theoretically part of the religious establishment now, I still have a lot to say about the church and how it connects us to God—and how for many of us, it doesn't.

This book isn't for everyone. But it is for a lot of us, whether we want to admit it or not.

To begin with, let's talk about the fact that I said *in the subtitle* that this book is for heathens. (We won't talk about the fact that after seeing that, *you* picked it up and began reading.)

Merriam-Webster defines *heathen* like this: (1) "of or relating to people or nations that do not acknowledge the God of the Bible," and (2) "strange, uncivilized."

So am I calling you a heathen? Of course not—but yeah, kind of. Technically speaking, there are *a lot* of customs and rituals that twenty-first-century Christians

1

don't do or even believe in. And thank God for that! Some of the customs of the religion that is in our Bible are at best outdated and at worse barbaric. Most Christians of the twenty-first century would be considered heathens by refined people in pretty much any other era. On top of that, we have that troublesome phrase, "the God of the Bible." Now which God would that be? There are as many definitions of God as there are people on the planet. Truth be told, they are probably (at least in part) wrong. St. Augustine said, "If you can conceive it, it's not God." There are *a lot* of interpretations of God in the Bible I don't acknowledge, and that probably goes for you too.

The second definition of heathen is "strange" and "uncivilized." OK, guilty as charged. I am calling you that. But that's a good thing (at least the strange part). I think we need now, more than ever, people who are willing to not fit in, people who are not down with the "one size fits all" of church. Or of anything! You picked up this book probably because the current way you are connecting to God (or not connecting) just feels . . . off. It's not an easy fit, it's off-kilter, it's a bit of a square-peg-in-a-round-hole situation. It's not necessarily *bad*. Just off.

This book is for people who are cynical about, fed up with, or simply uninspired by church as usual. They're good people who manage to live pretty moral lives. (Granted, "pretty moral" is relative.) I would even go so far as to call them, at times, saints. Nelson Mandela said, "I am not a saint, unless you think of a saint as a sinner that keeps on trying."[1] The readers of this book are people who want to, somehow, keep on trying. They don't need weekly tips from a preacher. They can spot a sermon that has an opening, three points, and a close—with a few *Chicken Soup for the Soul* illustrations thrown in.

They know the tricks preachers sometimes use of throwing in a "In the original Greek . . ." or a "I was reading in the *New Yorker* the other day." (Make no mistake—I have done both these things. They aren't bad. But the listener craves something else.) Does this sound like you? Maybe you continue to go to church even though it just seems blah. You want more. You *need* more. You want that feeling of connection to something bigger—God? A community? A mission to change the world? Isn't that what this Jesus thing is supposed to be about?

Sadly, there are times when I feel like the people in the pews get it better than the leaders in the church do.

I do believe it's better than it was! At some point we have to own the fact that the church has done some horrific shit in the name of God. Many times we got it wrong. We've got to own that—and then move forward so that history doesn't repeat itself.

To be fair, I think most of us got off on a really bad foot when it comes to religion. The idea of original sin screwed us up pretty good. I think it is a colossal mind-screw to say that we started off in the hole and that we suck. First off, I don't think that was the beginning or "original" moment anyway. (It's not even in the Bible. Anywhere.) If we are going to start at the beginning, then let's start *at* the beginning! We *start* with, as Richard Rohr, Matthew Fox, and others like to call it, "original blessing." That I can be down with. In the beginning it was good, good, good, until God created people and then—wait for it—it was *very* good! Now *that* sounds like good news.

We are learning that shaming is bad (duh) and that it never leads to change. (Not to mention that it was *never* done by Jesus—but I'll get back to him later.) I want this book to alleviate guilt, create joy, and give people permission to find God in new and different ways—even if that means sleeping in on Sundays.

I know of what I speak. Sunday morning worship services were never the happiest hour of my week. Even when I was an altar boy at St. Raphael's in metro Detroit, it just was not my gig. Having said that, I knew I loved God! Sunday mornings still aren't great—I'm not afraid to say it—and I'm a pastor! I know a lot of pastors who dread Sunday morning. They get it. They want it to be better, they know it isn't working, and yet they don't know what to do about it. I couldn't live like that. Once I had put in enough time "paying my dues," and had bugged the right people enough, I got to start my own thing. I kinda said to hell with Sunday mornings. Not just because it wasn't working for *me*, but I knew it wasn't working for a lot of people. To this day—and I love my colleagues—I have not found a church to go to since I started my faith community eight years ago.

People don't really know what to call AfterHours. The people who actually *go* to AfterHours call it a church. But the people in the "business" of church (professional church people) always call it a "ministry." "Your ministry is so . . . unique," they say. It's like the minute we started feeding homeless people every week, we apparently stopped being a church.

I'll take being a ministry—and a church.

Our gathering time, which I and others call happy hour (OK, maybe just me) is literally happy hour (well, almost—we meet at seven o'clock. If you are still at happy hour at 7 p.m., you aren't at happy hour anymore—you are on your way to getting drunk. Call Uber). We meet in bars, we eat, we drink, we chat about life and God and Jesus, and we make lunches to feed our homeless neighbors. And the folks who come are just like you. They are what I like to call spiritual independents: They are done with playing the church game; they just want to connect with other real people with real issues and do some real good in the world. They don't need a steeple and sermon to do that—and neither do you.

Kelly, one of the people on my leadership team, is agnostic, and she knows more about how the church runs than anyone I know. (She's flown across the country to study church administration. She knows her shit.) She is also one of the most loving people I know—that "Don't just say it, but roll up your sleeves and show it" kind of love. I'll take her over a thousand Christians who sit passively by and just point fingers.

I want to be clear from the get-go: I am not here to bash church. I am here to bash shitty church—and I think God would agree. (I can back up this claim with some Bible stuff, but that comes later.) It is actually the fact that I *do* care about church that leads me to make some of these comments. I think church can save this world—if we can figure out a way to do it right and in a meaningful way, if we can figure out how to serve the community and the planet and get on board with people who want to change the world and put more love into it.

Connection is the key. I think the desire to connect to something bigger is strong, even hardwired. We are born to be in community—authentic community, though, not one forced upon us. I think we also long to be a part of something that helps change the world for good. This can be feeding the poor, running a 5K to end cancer, or planting a tree. We want more. We want to feel that we matter. When we feel that connection to something bigger, whether it's a community or a cause, well, it's awesome.

And that is the goal for this book: to help you discover your bigger thing. The thing Søren Kierkegaard called "the idea for which I can live and die."

I think religion can give us the framework, but I don't think it's necessarily a house everybody wants (or frankly, needs) to live in. Community and a connection to something higher can take *a lot* of forms.

If you have a faith community that you are digging like a ditch, put this book down and go be a part of it. (If you already bought the book, pass it on to someone who needs it.) But if you don't have that community, if you don't have that "thing," then read on.

I think you might pick up what I'm puttin' down.

I'm going to introduce you to the religious misfits and rogue disciples who make up our tiny, faithful, ass-kicking AfterHours community. I will be talking about Heather, who invited all of AfterHours to her burlesque class "final," and how the group left her teacher speechless. I will be talking about Adam, who has two full sleeves of tattoos (many of which are visual illustrations of Bible passages . . . and one of which is one of our AfterHours logos!), and what drew him back to community after having been hurt by it years ago. I will be talking about our beautiful LGBTQ folks who give us a beauty and authenticity that we would have never had if they had not come to help teach us how to live in our own skin. I have learned from them that sometimes we need to walk away from communities and "friends" who don't accept us for who we are. (Who can't relate to that?)

I will also be telling stories from the park, where we hand out sack lunches and do Communion every day. These are stories of hope and healing and of the homeless who make me forget about my own stupid self-absorption and help me remember that there are people with problems *way* bigger than the fact that my wife, Laura, bought the wrong kind of cream cheese and the fact that we are running out of room in our fridge and had better "eat it up" this week. (*Then* I get pissed because I don't get to eat out as much.) Basically, the homeless of my community remind me I can be a whiny little bitch.

See, in this book, I don't really care if you "go to church" or not. I really don't.

But man, I do care a lot that you find your "thing." I really do care if you connect to something bigger than yourself and find a community of people who love you. I care a helluva lot that you find a way to stop searching for meaningless shit and instead find something that feeds your spirit and your soul. I care more than you know that you find that thing that Howard Thurman said "makes you come alive."

If even one of you finds your way, or your direction, or your compass, or your peeps as a result of reading these words, it will all be worth it.

I start every chapter with a section called "The Spirituality of . . ." In these sections (and sprinkled throughout chapters), you will find stories of people who found their connection to something bigger through what might be considered "nontraditional avenues": surfing, yoga, riding horses, even a good cigar. The purpose of these sections is to help you expand your understanding of connection to the holy by adding some roads that traditionally haven't been associated with the sacred. In short, we want to get God out of the box that we stuck God in in the first place.

Oh, and there might be drink recipes at the end of every chapter. I was a bartender for ten years when I first started off in stand-up comedy. Enjoying a well-made cocktail is one of the great joys of my life. I might as well pass on my knowledge to you. These are marked "for heathens' eyes only."

Before I go any further, I need to offer a huge disclaimer: It goes without saying (but I'm going to say it anyway) that *alcohol has created havoc in many people's lives throughout history. It has ruined lives and families and has parted people with their money time and time again since the beginnings of history.*

So has religion.

But it is not alcohol or religion that has done this destruction. It is the misuse of these tools. Alcohol and religion in and of themselves aren't dangerous. But their careless use can destroy.

So if you are a person who finds a good drink enriching to the soul, on with the cocktails.

FOR HEATHENS' EYES ONLY

Old Fashioned

2 dashes Angostura bitters
1 sugar cube
    (1 tsp. sugar = 1 sugar cube = 1 sugar packet)
2 oz. rye or bourbon

I use the New York City area code of 212 to remember the recipe: 2 dashes, 1 cube, 2 oz. It's three moves. People tend to overthink this drink. Put sugar and bitters in a glass (muddle if using a sugar cube). Add a few ice cubes and the booze. Stir. Add a lemon or orange slice. Enjoy.

Chapter One

Things God Does (and Doesn't) Care About

THE SPIRITUALITY OF . . . YOGA

"One of the benefits I have found from yoga is I haven't killed my children," says Amanda Henderson.

We parents get it. The fact that Amanda has two teenagers and one more approaching that stage and that she works what feels like a hundred hours a week doing justice work as the executive director of the Interfaith Alliance of Colorado means that it is not only a benefit to do yoga but a necessity.

This is not Amanda's first yoga rodeo. She has been doing yoga for more than twenty-five years, and she still catches herself feeling awkward sometimes. "But I've found it has helped me become comfortable being awkward, both in the studio and out in the world." Yes, she has gotten comfortable being uncomfortable.

"It has helped me lean into uncomfortableness and not shy away from it," she told me over breakfast tacos and frittatas in a hip coffeehouse in South Denver.

Amanda does a lot of work around injustice; sexism, racism, nativism, and inequality are the waters in which she swims. It can be stressful and painful and just not very fun.

Yoga on a daily basis allows her to "hit the reset button," as she puts it, every morning.

It allows her to be in a community where she can share a common experience and not have to deal with the occasional awkwardness of small talk. "We are a community that has this shared experience, and many times I don't even know the names of the people on the mat next to me. It allows me to share in a community in a different way besides just sitting in a pew."

When I asked her how in other ways it differs from the church experience, she was quick to mention the physicality of it. "I don't like to sit still—in a pew or elsewhere." Yoga allows her to connect to something bigger, not just with her mind and heart, but with her body and soul. "Jesus was incarnate. He became a physical being and used himself completely. He touched people, he healed people. He understood the power of touch."

Amanda says, "[Yoga has been] especially useful to help me heal after particularly difficult times." Focusing on her body and being aware of how it connects to others and the larger world brings a sort of healing that's different from simply "talking through" hard things. "It [is] healing without using words."

Yoga has also taught her about the cycles of life. "In yoga you do a hard position, then rest, then try to push yourself even harder, then rest again, then try to push yourself as hard and as far as you can, and then rest." She said it serves as a reminder that the rest of her life can benefit from this as well.

"Life moves in cycles. Yoga helps remind me of this."

I have to believe that God wants us to live in joy. God wants us to, and I quote, "have life and have it abundantly." (That's John 10:10.) That sounds like a pretty good gig to me.

If we find ourselves suffering through an hourlong worship service, I am pretty certain that is not the joy train. (Again, if you are digging it—I mean *really* digging it—that's *awesome*. Carry on. Nothing to see here.) But nothing is sadder to me than going to a service with a "rockin'" praise band (eye roll) only to see the congregation with their limp arms halfway raised and weakly "praising God." We can do better! We can all see it ain't real, and we can all feel it. It is heartbreaking to everyone involved—especially God. (If Santa knows when we are sleeping and when we're awake, don't you think God sure as hell knows when we're phoning it in?)

So what do we do? I certainly don't want to throw the baby out with the bathwater. Like I said earlier, this is *not* about church bashing. But it is about *bad church* bashing. I've got nothing against church done well. That does not necessarily mean jumbo screens and huge stages and lighting boards. Complex and fancy isn't what pleases God. In fact, there is something beautiful about a simple service straight out of a hymnal, but that's no good either if our heart's not in it. Shouldn't we all be against a lousy product when the product is our gift to God? God deserves our whole heart, and at the very least our honest feelings, right?

Somewhere, somehow, we got the idea that the most important thing for Christians to do is to get together in a certain place, on a certain day, at a certain time, and sing love songs to our boyfriend Jesus. Now don't get me wrong—again, I think gathering together is essential for community, but sometimes the services I have gone to on Sunday morning are so sterile that there is almost no way for people to form genuine connection. They are more like a board meeting with songs sprinkled in—and an offering. We can't forget the offering.

This is not to say that music isn't important, but I think it has to be *felt* even more than heard.

Todd Seeleu is a pastor who is hiding out in a rock-and-roll band. Actually, it's more of an outlaw country band . . . that likes to play the blues. Todd is the drummer for the band Next 2 the Tracks. They tour all over the country and have played more than a few biker parties. And these are not like "your friends who get together to ride bikes on the weekend and who are dentists during the week" bikers. They are more like the Bandidos of Texas, one of the largest motorcycle clubs in the country. Todd looks more like a bouncer who would work the door than a reverend with a doctorate in ministry.

Besides touring, Todd also believes being in bars and clubs is his ministry. (Yeah right, no one will buy *that!*) He does church services in bars in New Mexico. They play music, read a bit of the Bible, drink a few beers, and talk about God. It works.

I sat down with Todd and a few beers at an upstairs bar in Denver between gigs on the road and his church gatherings. He believes he can find God in the music, and he's not talking about gospel choirs. He's talking about rock band Tool. "I started listening to the lyrics and realized this music was connecting me to God and something bigger than a lot of church experiences I had been involved in." I asked him whether it's possible he's making it something bigger than it is. What would he say to people who claim he just likes that music and is not really connecting to God through it? Without missing a beat, he said, "I would say they're listening to shitty music."

Music, like almost nothing else, gives us the instantaneous power to be moved to another place, even if that place isn't an actual, physical place. It transports us and moves us right from the depths of our soul. Yet it is almost impossible to explain. As Maynard James Keenan, the lead singer of Tool, said, "You really should be able to feel the higher power of the music and be moved by it, rather than listening to me waffle on and having to explain it."[1]

So when did many churches make the switch from feeling worship to doing worship? We certainly didn't get this model from the early church. We only have to look as far as Acts 2. That community sounded like a group that gathered together to love and serve others and each other. Let's look a little deeper at what those first communities were like and what their purpose and mission were.

"I'm Sorry, but I Just Got Tired of Your Worship"—God

God basically sends religious people a "Dear John" letter—also known as "It's not me, it's you." You can find several versions of this sentiment throughout the Bible: Amos 5:21–24; Isaiah 1:13–14, 17; Rev. 3:15–17; and Matt. 23:23–28, to name a few.

Throughout the Old and New Testaments we see a God who, at times, has grown weary of people worshiping her. (By the way, sometimes I will refer to God as *her*, sometimes *him*. I think God is gender neutral, but that can be too much for our small brains to deal with, so for the sake of gender equality, I use both.) In these moments we see a God who has the same look on his face that most of us do while watching a really bad sixth-grade play. And that's if we are lucky. In other passages it's a God who is downright *angry*—like, yelling and screaming and thinking about throwing a lightning bolt our way. Why? Because God doesn't care about your worship if you're not also practicing love and justice!

It's clear that religious people don't—and never did—have a monopoly on justice, mercy, humility, or love. And as you've probably noticed, in many cases the church seems to be lacking those things severely. That may be why you left church in the first place. If so, you will be glad to know that the reasons you don't like church are the very same reasons God doesn't either! (At least, that's what God told us in the Bible.) To be clear, it isn't that God doesn't like church. It's that God doesn't like hollow, empty, shiny-on-the outside-but-ugly-on-the-inside church.

After a quick gander at these passages, the average person who is fed up with Sunday worship won't feel so alone. Apparently, based on these passages, we have been doing bad church for millennia!

Before we go on, though, I must say a word about quoting Bible passages. I know that the reason we do that is so others can find the quote later and check our work. It is meant as a favor to those reading or listening for their studies down the road. That is mostly crap, however. The Bible is the best-selling book in the world *and* the least-read book in 90 percent of the homes it is in. I have so many Bibles I don't even know where they all are. While the quoting of Scripture is stated as a helpful thing, I think that more often than not it comes out as self-righteous and holier than thou. Many times it's condescending and flat-out rude, intended to shut down a conversation rather than open one up. The passages I'm quoting here are not to make you feel like shit if you don't know them, but rather to show you that if you struggle with the church as an organized institution that is hell-bent on self-preservation among all other things and the hypocrisy of that makes your stomach turn like it just got off a Tilt-A-Whirl, then good news! You aren't alone! God is standing right with you, equally bummed out and appalled.

Now, on with quoting the Bible. And if you don't read the Bible or believe in God, that's cool. Read on anyway. These are probably not passages any of your churchgoing friends have heard quoted in church—ever. Next time you see them, *you* can quote *them* a passage.

Amos 5:21–24

I hate, I despise your festivals,
    and I take no delight in your solemn assemblies.
Even though you offer me your burnt offerings and
      grain offerings,
    I will not accept them;
and the offerings of well-being of your fatted animals
    I will not look upon.
Take away from me the noise of your songs;
    I will not listen to the melody of your harps.
But let justice roll down like waters,
    and righteousness like an ever flowing stream.

Here in Amos we see a God who isn't interested in high holidays or sober gatherings. Amos was a prophet. While that might *sound* like a cool job, most prophets didn't fare well in the Bible. Their job was to bring a message from God, and often, God was pissed. As a result, a lot of them were far from popular. In Amos's case, he called the people out on their worship. The idea of offerings was so offensive that God wouldn't even look at them, let alone accept them. She was not even interested in the choir!

So what does interest God in this passage? Justice. Righteousness. What does righteousness mean in the

Bible? Ethical conduct. *Conduct*—not what we believe or what we say we believe. It is about how we act. How are our ethics and conduct woven into the fabric of our lives? This matters a great deal to God. It is the act of living life with justice and righteousness that gets God's attention. Pursuing justice means asking this question: What systems do we have in place that contribute to abundant life, and what systems do we have that increase human suffering? The systems that lead to abundant life make up what is known to many as the kingdom of God. Those systems that lead to human suffering need to be eliminated.

My brother Gene died in 2001. At his funeral, his son Kelly quoted an often-used phrase of Gene's: "Don't tell me what ya gonna do. Tell me what ya done." Ideas and plans and intentions are great, but it is in the doing that the value lies.

Isaiah 1:13–14, 17

Bringing offerings is futile;
　　incense is an abomination to me.
New moon and sabbath and calling of convocation—
　　I cannot endure solemn assemblies with iniquity.
Your new moons and your appointed festivals
　　my soul hates;
they have become a burden to me,
　　I am weary of bearing them.
. . . .
　　Learn to do good;
seek justice,
　　rescue the oppressed,
defend the orphan,
　　plead for the widow.

Once again we see a God who is just over it when it comes to offerings and taking a day of rest and celebrations. God can't endure solemn assemblies. Another way to read this is that God can't stand boring church!

But all is not lost. God does throw us a bone to give us an idea of what *does* matter to her. We see the list here: do good, seek justice, rescue the oppressed, defend the orphan, plead for the widow. That alone would keep us busy for a good long while.

To be clear, God is not talking about *just* widows and orphans to defend and plead for. He is using first-century shorthand. Widows and orphans were considered almost less than people in biblical times. They were, as we like to say these days, on the margins. This means that they had almost no voice and no power in society. Women and children in general had little to no power, but to take away a woman's husband or a child's parents? Then the only advocate they *might* have had is gone. They aren't helpless, but they're damn close. God is telling us here to get off our asses and help those who at this moment can use a little help.

Thank God we live in a different day. Women have more of a voice (though still not nearly enough), and there are entire nonprofits dedicated to speaking for and caring for children. Despite how it might feel at times, more people have more voice than ever before. And that's how God wants it. (I will speak more to this in the coming chapter.)

Revelation 3:15–17

I know your works; you are neither cold nor hot. I wish that you were either cold or hot. So, because you are lukewarm, and neither cold nor hot, I am

> about to spit you out of my mouth. For you say, "I am rich, I have prospered, and I need nothing." You do not realize that you are wretched, pitiable, poor, blind, and naked.

OK, God, tell us how you really feel.

Here we see a God who is not impressed by us sitting around when there is so much work to be done. God loves passion! God is not pleased when we claim to have no opinion, to not be for or against, when we stay in the middle and stay quiet about important things. *Your voice matters.* This idea that to sit idly by is "OK" is a fallacy. Desmond Tutu said, "If you are neutral in situations of injustice, you have chosen the side of the oppressor." Similarly, human rights activist Ginette Sagan said, "Silence in the face of injustice is complicity with the oppressor."

We were not made to sit around rich and prosperous and in need of nothing. If and when any of us get to that place, we are called to reach back and help those who are not there yet. And we don't have to wait till then either!

Take action. Show passion. Get off the fence.

Matthew 23:23–28

> Woe to you, scribes and Pharisees, hypocrites! For you tithe mint, dill, and cummin, and have neglected the weightier matters of the law: justice and mercy and faith. It is these you ought to have practiced without neglecting the others. You blind guides! You strain out a gnat but swallow a camel!
>
> Woe to you, scribes and Pharisees, hypocrites! For you clean the outside of the cup and of the plate, but inside they are full of greed and self-indulgence.

You blind Pharisee! First clean the inside of the cup, so that the outside also may become clean.

Woe to you, scribes and Pharisees, hypocrites! For you are like whitewashed tombs, which on the outside look beautiful, but inside they are full of the bones of the dead and of all kinds of filth. So you also on the outside look righteous to others, but inside you are full of hypocrisy and lawlessness.
Woe to you, scribes and Pharisees, hypocrites! For you build the tombs of the prophets and decorate the graves of the righteous. . . .

"Woe to you." Jesus uses that a lot here—four times in six verses, and seven times in all (which is the biblical number of completion or perfection). The Greek word translated "woe" means more than just how someone feels. It is a judgment. Same thing in Hebrew. Jesus used the word *woe* more than anyone else in the Bible. And who does he reserve the word for here? Scribes and Pharisees! Damn! The very people who wrote and interpreted the law. Jesus saw that they *knew* the law but that they just didn't follow it themselves. Jesus' response reminds me of the words of the prophet Marvin the Martian: "You have made me very, very angry—very angry indeed."

Jesus calls the scribes and Pharisees *hypocrites*. This word comes from the Greek term for actor or someone who wears a mask. Such people profess to believe one thing but act to the contrary. The fact that Jesus uses this term over and over emphasizes how important it is to Jesus that our words follow our actions. To say the words and not to live them out makes Jesus very, very angry— very angry indeed.

The idea that any people or institutions look one way on the outside and are completely different on the inside is not pleasing to God. It's called hypocrisy. We are all guilty of it to one degree or another, and yet we hate it in others. And God is never pleased with it. Again, we are back to "How are you living out your life?" This seems to be a more important litmus test for Jesus and God than your attendance record at church or how much of the Bible you have memorized.

Why ARE People Going to Church?

If God is so critical of worship, why do people keep going to church? If even the one being worshiped sees it as empty and hypocritical, why do people even bother? Too many people have bought the lie that if you don't go to church, pray certain prayers, or participate in certain rituals, God will send you to hell.

Before trying to debunk the reasons God would send a person to hell, I guess I should start by saying I don't believe in hell in the first place. Rob Bell said the same thing and had his ass handed to him, but as he would be quick to tell you, he is not the first theologian to adhere to this belief (and I sure as hell won't be the last). A belief in hell wasn't even part of the dominant Christian thinking until the fourth or fifth century.

There are a lot of reasons why I don't believe in hell. First, *Sheol* and *Hades*, Hebrew and Greek words often translated as "hell," are considered by most scholars to mean "grave" and not a place of punishment and torture. (In Greek mythology, Hades was the god of the underworld.) Sheol and Hades are places of darkness and silence. Second, the idea of "eternal conscious torment" (as hell's biggest fans like to say) flies in the face of grace.

Period. Even when Jesus mentions "eternal fire" in Matthew 25 and in Revelation as a place where God's enemies end up, I have to believe these are illustrations. I don't think Jesus was being literal. Who among us would sentence even their *worst enemy* to an eternity of torture? Who is psychopathic enough to do something like that? God? *Really?*

Don't we think that God is at least as compassionate and loving as we are? And if he isn't, why would we follow that God? (I love Marcus Borg's line to atheists: "Tell me about the God you don't believe in. I probably don't believe in that God either.")

In the end, I don't believe in hell because it flies in the face of who I believe God to be. The God I believe in is love, and eternal torment simply isn't in that God's nature. Love will always win against vengeance.

To be clear, not everyone who goes to church does so out of fear or guilt. Some (I might even say many) who go genuinely love the community, the music, the preaching, and the ritual. This chapter is not for them.

This chapter is for people who don't go a lot (or ever) and for whom that causes even just the slightest tinge of guilt—or, depending on how often you talk to your mom, a lot of guilt. I want to absolve you of that guilt. You're not going to hell for spending your Sunday mornings at Starbucks with a nice latte and that special someone, or in a yoga class, or at home reading a book. You can have a vibrant spiritual life without the Sunday morning ordeal. I am certain that one-on-one conversations can be deeply, deeply spiritual. So can moving your body. So can sitting or reading quietly all by oneself.

There's a lot to be said for solitude. Now I know some people who might snicker that someone as extroverted and outgoing as I am would advocate for solo time. These are people who generally want to put people in a box, label them one thing, shut the box, and think they know those people. Not cool. We have to own the fact that alone time can look a lot different to different people.

For me, it's cigars. I understand if the idea of a cigar being spiritual might be ridiculous to you. I understand if you think it is no more than an ugly habit. I understand that for some, the idea of putting cigar smoking in the same category as evening vespers might feel insulting to evening vespers. So be it. And yes, I know cigars aren't good for me. But I like almost everything about them. Granted, I don't like the way they make my clothes smell—which is why I have cigar-smoking clothes. For one thing, I like the ritual of smoking a cigar. I like using the cutter and using the lighter. I like the process of getting a cigar lit "right." I like that first draw, and I like how when I exhale I can feel the stress leaving my body with my breath. I like staring out into the darkness. (I almost always smoke alone, at night, on my porch.) I like how it forces me to do nothing else.

I know guys who smoke while they golf or take walks or are out on a boat. I'm not that guy. I either smoke alone at night, or during the day with a friend like Brian or Eric. I can't remember when I have smoked with more than one person. For me, it is not an activity that lends itself to a crowd. It's just me, or just me and a friend—usually someone who has no trouble going into deep conversation, someone who is not scared of the big questions. Whether I am with someone or not, cigar smoking is my time for pondering big questions. I actually don't even care about the answers. Their power is in the asking.

I usually smoke Robusto cigars. According to *Cigar Aficionado*, it is the most popular size cigar in America. It is about five inches long and has a ring gauge (measurement around the cigar) of between 48 and 52. It usually can last around thirty to forty minutes, which is perfect for me. That is enough time for me to contemplate life, but not so much that I am sitting there so long I go to a dark place. Plus, like most people, I've got shit to do.

I find that while it doesn't "fix me" or get me to a place of total clarity, it does help me reboot. It almost always leads me to gratitude. It slows my mind and my breathing and my heart rate. In those moments, even if I'm technically all alone, I know that God is with me.

That reminder doesn't suck either.

Sometimes that kind of deep contemplation is hard to do in a church service, which is full of words and scripted events. But one thing a lot of churches do supply is community, something people crave whether or not organized religion is their thing. I know that a huge percentage of the people who go to AfterHours don't go for what I have to say. I think there are some that don't even come for the opportunity to make PB&Js (although I do think that ties for first). I think most come for community, and everything falls in line after that. That's what the faith community in Acts 2 seemed to be all about, and it sounds like a pretty decent way to do the church thing. That chapter of Acts describes how the people of that community ate together in each other's homes, met together every day, shared what they had, and sold stuff they had so they could give to others outside their community who were in need.

I am not suggesting we take things to that extreme (though some people today do choose to live like this in what they call "intentional community"), but I do believe we can take these elements, work them into our communities, and become better communities for it.

So What DOES God Care About?

Obviously, you can still go to church on Sunday morning if that's your thing. But it's not God's deal breaker if you don't. (Pro tip: God can tell when we're faking it.) Let's look at what exactly God *does* want from us. As luck would have it, God gave us CliffsNotes. It's in a couple of places (I don't think God wanted us to miss it), such as Micah 6:8 in the Hebrew Bible (what Christians call the Old Testament):

> He has shown you, O mortal, what is good.
>   And what does the Lord require of you?
> To act justly and to love mercy
>   and to walk humbly with your God.

Let's "unpack that" (a pretentious little phrase I learned in seminary and want to pass on to you the reader) and take a closer look at what God wants from us (actually, *requires* is the word). Let's also look at what is *not* mentioned. The church doesn't have a monopoly on justice, mercy, humility, or love. You can have them too—and probably already do.

Three things—that's all God gives us here. (It is in response to Israel asking God if burnt offerings and other goodies would be enough to satisfy God.) God says not to worry about dead calves and tankers full of oil. These things are meaningless and certainly not "required."

God wants us to act justly, but not in the worldly sense of justice. You do something bad, you get punished. That's retributive justice—the flavor of justice that about 99.9 percent of the world is interested in. This does not interest God. God is more interested in restorative justice—being remade whole, putting broken things back together. This is the kind of acting justly that God wants to see happen. How do we not punish, but, rather, fix and make whole again?

Then God tells us to love mercy. Notice that God does not just tell us to *do* mercy, but to *love* it. Mercy, compassion, love—these are the hallmarks of how we should be living our lives and that should be filling our hearts and minds.

Finally, God wants us to walk humbly with him. I love how the verse tells us to walk *with*, to be in relationship. This is at the core of God's desire: to be in relationship together. I think walking humbly with God also means that, over time, we find ourselves caring about others more and more and ourselves less and less. We find ourselves willing to be selfless more and more. This is not about thinking less of ourselves, but rather putting more and more time into the love and care of others.

The second set of CliffsNotes is in Matthew 22:36–40. Here is what Jesus said when a lawyer asked him a question:

> "Teacher, which commandment in the law is the greatest?" He said to him, "'You shall love the Lord your God with all your heart, and with all your soul, and with all your mind.' This is the greatest and first commandment. And a second is like it: 'You shall love your neighbor as yourself.' On these two commandments hang all the law and the prophets."

That's all! Good night, folks! Tip your server! Be careful going home!

Seriously, Jesus? Nowhere do you mention my twelve-part summer preaching series on the Ten Commandments? What the hell?

I love how throughout the Bible, Jesus keeps circling back to simple stuff: love, grace, forgiveness, acceptance. In essence, the Bible comes down to "Be kind." Oh sure, I know what the scholars, and my snootier colleagues, and those who want to make any of us feel small would say to that: "But Jerry, you are missing so much! The Bible is so much more layered and complex and rich than 'just don't be mean.'" I want layered, complex, and rich in my cheesecake, not my theology. The best lines I have heard, and learned, and remembered, and tried to live out have always been simple: "Do no harm," "Love God, love people," "Practice kindness," "Do unto others," "Judge not," "Don't be an asshole." Putting these simple truths into practice might take a hundred different forms: feeding the poor, protesting injustice, caring for the sick, offering a kind word, and a lot more. But they all fall under that umbrella of showing kindness to others.

We can miss this when we are so busy pointing out how others are doing it "not right." I know when I start to complain about how others are "not getting it right," it is nine times out of ten my own shit. If we just focus on loving people—particularly those who seem unlovable—I think we will end up in pretty good shape. It's funny to me how many people dismiss "loving people," how many want to make it more complicated. I sometimes wonder if the devil's underlying intention is for us to stay mired in dialogue about what it really means to "love people." That way, if we are busy debating it, we never *really* have to get around to doing it. (Note: I don't believe in the devil.)

A number of AfterHours people, while probably not atheists, are pretty solidly in the agnostic camp. They are also some of the most solid Christians I know. Now *they* wouldn't call themselves that, but if you define a Christian as someone who lives like Jesus and treats others the way Jesus did, they win! Mandie, who lives her life with joy and kindness, cares for others and hates injustice. Check, check, check! She did a fundraiser *on her own* and handed AfterHours a four-figure check—and she doesn't believe in church! As my lifelong atheist friend Michelle said, "I don't believe in the God stuff—I believe in the good stuff." Ironically, I think Michelle and Mandie's beliefs in this category fall into line with those of Jesus. If we have to narrow it down to two words, they are this: Love people.

Some people might object to that, since, after all, Jesus also said, "Love God." That's true, but how exactly do you love God?

I think we take it out of the mysterious and put it into the real and the tangible: How do you love God? Well, how do you love people?

I remember reading somewhere the simple way to get this right: "Love God, love people. If you want to know how well you are doing the first one, look at how well you are doing the second."

Sallie McFague, an American feminist Christian theologian who was born in the early 1930s, puts it this way:

> We cannot love God unless we love God's world. Christians [should] have always known this, because an incarnate God is a world-loving God; but now it takes on new meaning and depth as we realize the radical interrelationship and interdependence of all forms of life. . . . In sum, we are not called to love God or the world. Rather, we are called to love God in the world. We love God by loving the world. We love God through and with the world. But this turns out to be a kenotic, a sacrificial love.[2]

I think that's the way we show God love—through the way we treat other people and our interaction with them. Sometimes we may feel alone, like no one's there and, to be completely honest, like God's not there either. Even though people say that God is always with you, if you don't feel it, does it matter? Is it real? For some, God is the proverbial tree falling in the forest with no one around. I think sometimes that's because we are looking in the wrong places.

Sometimes I think, "Well, I don't know if I really saw God tonight, but I had a really good conversation with John, it was excellent talking to Rebekah, and Adam was there and we had a really deep talk. They helped me with some dark stuff I was working through."

Well, maybe I did see God. Maybe it wasn't in the "clouds parting and James Earl Jones speaking from above" kind of way. Maybe it was in Rebekah listening when I needed an ear, Adam saying, "You're doing great; keep it up," or John just giving me a hug—a real hug—and reminding me I'm loved.

That's God.

Teresa of Avila, a Spanish mystic and saint from the 1500s, was widely attributed to have said, "Christ has no body now but yours. No hands, no feet on earth but yours. Yours are the eyes through which he looks with compassion on this world." We are the hands, feet, and eyes of Christ—and, I think, the ears and the mouth—and God speaks through us. What we say and think and do regarding others matters!

I think we make loving God too damn big a deal. Too mysterious, I mean. Too intangible. I think most people believe we've got to be on our knees, praying the rosary, diving into the Bible, and memorizing passages. I don't think so.

I'm a big, big fan of loving God, and I think prayers are great, but as with any relationship, we can't just say over and over, "I love you, I love you, I love you," and then treat the other person like shit. After a while, the other person will start to wonder if they believe us anymore.

I think God is much more interested in how we love other people than in what specific flavor or denomination of religion we belong to or even if we belong to any. How we treat others *is* how we pray to God. I think if I were given the choice between somebody saying "I love you" all the time and treating me like crap, or actually loving me through their actions but never saying it, I would take the actions without words every time.

I think about how someone might treat my son Hudson. If you want to show you love me or care about me, then treat my kid with kindness.

I think it's the same way with God: Treat my kids well. That's how I know you love me.

We so often desperately try to separate ourselves from others and God, to be rugged individualists. The truth is that *we are all connected.* This connectedness is a wisdom that has gone down through the ages across multiple traditions and religions. All those interactions have a direct effect on others. And all the ways we interact with others is a direct interaction with God. For those who follow Jesus, it couldn't be made any plainer. This is one of the times Jesus really lays it out for us: "As you do to the least of my brothers, *you do to me.*" Folks, what else do we need? Skywriting and fireworks wouldn't be more obvious.

The hard part of that command, though, is "the least of my brothers." Damn it! I'm fine with treating people I like OK. I'm fine with being kind to those who are kind back. But *that guy*? He's a jerk! He's cocky and mean and arrogant and treats others like crap and is self-centered and self-absorbed and rude. He doesn't understand his privilege and has a huge ego and never gives to the poor, and he stepped on people to get where he's at. He's a tool and doesn't deserve my respect, and certainly not my love. To hell with that guy. You sure as hell can't mean *that* guy, Jesus.

"Yeah, I kinda do, actually—especially that guy."

Damn it! Being kind is hard. Sure is—but you said you want to love God, and that's what God wants for a present.

This to me is what separates the people who find that connection to something bigger from those who don't. It is hard to connect to the divine/the almighty/the universe/God and treat those around you like shit. I think there is a direct correlation between how we treat others and how well and how often we find that spark of the universe.

I think we can have an amazing time here on this planet. We can go to the best restaurants, climb the biggest mountains, visit the coolest cities, drive the best cars, and have the biggest homes, and, let's face it, that would be cool. We need to own that. Having and doing nice things would be, well, nice.

But it ain't gonna connect you to anything bigger. Only seeing the sunset will do that, or looking into the eyes of someone you love, or holding a newborn, or feeding someone in a food line.

The bigger things are not always the bigger things. Sometimes it is as simple as a gentle touch to feel in your soul a connection to the entire universe. It can be a fleeting moment, but in that moment you instantly feel that all is well. All hate and cruelty and ugliness fall away.

And all that is left is love.

FOR HEATHENS' EYES ONLY

Negroni

1 oz. gin
1 oz. Campari
1 oz. sweet vermouth (the red kind)

Pour each of these into a cocktail shaker (tin man) with ice. Stir many times. Strain into an old-fashioned glass with ice. Stir with your finger. Garnish with an orange slice. (David Wondrich suggests shaking with ice, but I say stick with the stirring. The drink isn't that hard either way, and you get your exercise in for the day.)

OR

Ride a Vespa to an outdoor cafe in Italy. Have them make you one. Stir it with your finger (I think this is a crucial part of the equation). The Negroni's been around since the 1860s. It's delicious and classy.

Chapter Two

Do Justice:
Service and Beyond

THE SPIRITUALITY OF . . . RUNNING

Running is about being present and opening your eyes to the world around you. It's about "lifting your head up" and seeing what is right in front of you. Sometimes running can be about running away from something, literally and metaphorically. Running is about touching the earth and realizing how amazing the world is.

I would love to tell you that these are my insights, but I don't really run unless I'm being chased (and thankfully, I was a good enough shoplifter in junior high that it never came to that). I have tried running more than once, but then I remember I hate running and turn around. It is usually within the first mile. I have learned that the first mile always sucks.

My friend Dottie Mann, on the other hand, loves running. Dottie is a chaplain and has been a runner for more than twenty years. She says it makes her feel alive. She knows a lot about being alive because she knows a lot about death. In her career as a chaplain, Dottie has held the hand of more than three hundred people as they left this world and went on to the next. Death doesn't scare her. Not living does.

Running started out being a "sanity check" for Dottie. "It clears my head," she says. She started running seriously when she had two small boys and her hour run was her only hour without small children around. Things would come into focus after a long run. And while she might not have answers, she has cleared the space for the answers to come. "Nothing else felt that good at the end of it."

It also proved to be good for dealing with grief after she lost Donna, one of her favorite running partners. "I discovered you cannot run and sob," she told me. You can run and cry, you can run and sniffle, but you can't run and sob. Sometimes I just stopped and sat down on the trail and sobbed my brains out."

While Dottie's job is "religion" professionally, she acknowledges that she, like most people, is really good at "talking to God" and less good at listening to God. While she would talk to God quite a bit on the trail, after a while she would find herself getting quiet. That is when she would hear God talking to her, through the beauty and the sounds and the feel of nature. "It didn't become intentionally spiritual for probably ten years," she said. But even before then, "it was subconsciously spiritual for me. It had to be, or I wouldn't have kept going."

When I asked her what she would say to someone who claimed that running is not spiritual but that she just likes it, she replied, "So if I like it, it can't be God? It can't be spiritual? Does God have to be found only on a creaky, cold, straightbacked pew? Spirituality is the pleasure of a rested mind, a calm soul."

I don't know about you, but I think we could all use more of that in our lives.

All of us, at our core, desire to be part of something bigger, deeper, more meaningful, and more important than just our own skin and bones. We are searching for meaning, for connection with something divine.

I think the number-one way to connect to the holy is to see it through the eyes of another human being. I also think we get bonus points for those eyes being different from ours and more bonus points if those eyes belong to someone who is poor and/or on the margins of our society and often gets the shitty end of the stick.

Simply put, I think finding a way to engage with the poor is the number-one way to encounter God. And don't just take my word for it. Ask any eighth-grader who has gone on a mission trip. Check any of the more than three hundred verses in the Bible that deal with our engagement with the poor. Ask anyone who has served the homeless in the park with AfterHours. Put simply, the poor are where it's at.

Even people who only have a passing knowledge of the Bible might have heard the statement "When I was hungry, you fed me, when I was thirsty, you gave me drink." Matthew 25 had it right. This passage goes on to say that whenever we do that for the least, we did it for Jesus. Now see? That doesn't suck! To know that every time I am encountering the poor, I am coming face-to-face with Jesus? What could be more badass than that!

I do believe that God loves us all. I do believe that we don't have to earn that love, and I think that if we close this book and do absolutely nothing different than we've been doing, God will love us exactly the same as if we cure cancer, climb Kilimanjaro, or win an Oscar. But if we want to feel closer to God, I think we need to own the fact that the poor are especially close to God's own heart. When we try to connect to those the rest of society has shit on, we are trying to connect to the very people Jesus got close to when he was here on earth.

I will not tell you that this is easy, and quite frankly, there are a lot of days I simply don't feel like it. I hate saying it because I sound like a tool, but there are days when I have just too much on my to-do list. Or feel I won't be "appreciated." Or I am just tired. Or I am burned out. It is not all sugarcoated unicorns. Sometimes helping the poor sucks.

But I will say this: I *always* feel better after I have done it—every single time. It's like going to the gym: you might not like going, but you are always glad you went. I think being with the poor works out our spiritual muscles. It makes our spirit stronger. And like working out, it can sometimes suck when you're in the middle of it.

Kelly Carver is a member of AfterHours who regularly goes to the park to feed our friends without homes. Kelly is a rock star in the park and is the proud owner of multiple tattoos. She is married to Adam, who is a welder and has, I am certain, lost track of how many tattoos he has. Kelly is an administrator at another Denver congregation, and she knows what's up with the church probably better than I do. But rather than just work there to get a paycheck, she steps up at least once a week and heads down to the park.

Kelly told me, "I had started attending AfterHours to find community and myself. I stayed when I found my people and realized that it felt like home. I started going to the park as part of the 'gig,' but I have kept going after five years because of Donald, Kenneth, Ronnie, Kathy, and so many others. Each time I go I am still shocked that there are human beings *living* outside. They sleep, eat, and go to the bathroom outside, or they travel a distance to a shelter or library that will let them stay for an hour. They have stories and pasts and futures and lives that nobody considers. I go to bring lunch, but more than that, I go—even when it is freezing and snowing—because they are outside and we may provide the only meal or interaction that someone gets in a day. I guess I go because we are all human, and I hope that if I am ever in a position that I live outdoors, someone will be there, no matter the day or weather."

And people without homes are only one group that God has called us to be with. Kelly and I and many others have heard too many people say too many times, "We don't have any homeless in our community, so it's really hard to find a way to serve." Service matters, no matter what kind. Aristotle once said that the essence of life is "to serve others and do good." Find anyone that society has pushed aside or kicked to the curb—as we say in my business, someone who is "on the margins." Who is on the margins? Anyone who doesn't get a fair shake in this world: immigrants; people of color; the poor; gay, lesbian, bisexual, and transgender people; people who are not able-bodied or have any kind of developmental impairment. These are the folks who are closest to God's heart. And while I think it would do all of us well to serve with and beside them, I think it is especially important for those of us who have benefited from our current society and systems. (Yes, I am looking at you, straight, able-bodied, white American male.) We have gotten every advantage the world has to give. Why not reach back and help someone get a little closer to their finish line?

Others before Self

Service is central to healing and recovery in the Alcoholics Anonymous community. I know a number of people in twelve-step programs, and they have told me that the act of service, no matter how small, is *huge* in the process of recovery.

My friend Tony (not his real name) is in AA. He has been sober for more than ten years. I asked him about AA's emphasis on service. "Service is key," he told me. "Service to others is a practice that minimizes the ego. Ego is the enemy of alcoholics." I told him that ego is the enemy of a lot of people (looking at myself here). He went on to say, "It's very difficult to pursue our own self-ishness when we try to keep service at the forefront." He remembered this quote from AA: "Our real purpose is to fit ourselves to be of maximum service to God and the people about us."

Sounds to me like advice that could work for all of us.

The truth is, we are all broken. We are all in various stages of recovery from *something*. Service breaks down our egos and helps us get outside ourselves. We lose our self-importance and self-centeredness and think about the other, if only for a minute. This goes for when we are handing out water in the park, making a PB&J, or empty-ing ashtrays at a twelve-step meeting.

This training helps us to look past superficial bull-shit like what kind of car the Joneses drive, what kind of jobs they have, and what kind of neighborhood they live in (which, I might add, is the root of so much of our suffering, mine included). The poor save me. They save me from my selfishness, my ego, my greed, my self-absorption, my vanity.

So, I'm on a diet. I don't love it, but without it, I am relatively certain I would be the size of a small to medium-size Airstream. One morning I was bummed that I was up a pound since the previous week—*a pound*. Meanwhile, around the globe 795 million people are suf-fering from chronic undernourishment. That's one in nine.[1] What kind of jackass complains that he must have eaten too much when one in nine don't have enough to live? Someone who is focused on himself, that's who. I went to load up a truck with some sleeping bags to hand out to folks without homes on Christmas Day. Guess what? I drove home laughing at myself for what a fool I was that morning before weighing in. Service does that.

Trying to see the world through marginalized eyes will change both us and those we serve. A 2013 Harvard study noted that volunteering is good for enhancing our mental and physical health, warding off loneliness and depression, lowering blood pressure, and contributing to a longer life span, yet we still don't seem to be getting the picture.[2] In 2014, *Newsweek* reported that the percentage of Americans volunteering had dwindled and was at its lowest level in a decade. In 2013, the volunteer rate was 25.4 percent, compared with 29 percent of the population in 2003, according to the U.S. Bureau of Labor Statistics.[3]

Let's be clear, though, that the poor are not here to make "us" feel good. I do not have a problem with feeling good as a result of doing good, but it has to be a by-product, never the main reason. Like anything, our service can become a source of vanity if we're not careful. It's easy to take on a messiah complex: "Don't worry, I'll come in and save the day!" This is *so* common among clergy. I am as guilty of it as anyone, if not more so. I have to be on the watch constantly for when I start to veer off into knight-in-shining-armor territory. This kind of "help" smacks of superiority and arrogance. And it is worse, because it is cloaked in good deeds.

Authentic, healthy work with others who are in need always recognizes and includes a give-and-take. It leaves all parties more whole and validated, and everybody leaves a bit better than they were when they got there.

Few things alleviate the hole that is in a lot of us more than getting outside of ourselves and reaching out in a way that says, "What do you need? How can I help? Is there anything I can do?" Begin each day asking these questions. Answer them in your own way—every day. Watch the change that occurs.

Moving beyond ourselves connects us to something bigger. Again, I don't believe this has to be a huge thing. I think every small win counts. Every action that puts others first we are going to put on the board. It doesn't have to be at a church. It doesn't have to be with the homeless. It doesn't have to be a big, huge deal. Every act has a ripple effect.

My friend Robin said it this way: "We are rocks. God throws us in the water. What kind of ripples are you creating?" I *love* that metaphor. Our actions matter, for good and bad. What are the ripples that you are causing? Are they for good or bad? Are your actions selfish or selfless? What are you putting out there?

In the end, we are talking about your soul. This is soul work. This is doing the small, consistent practices that, over time, will change our core and change who we are. I think the reverse is true too. The less we do to help others, the easier it is to become (or stay) a self-absorbed jackass.

Lately, I've been carrying a large brass coin in my pocket every day. On it is the inscription *Memento mori*. It is Latin for "Remember that you have to die." And while this sounds like a raging downer, it is actually just the opposite. It leads to the practice of reflecting on one's own mortality. This coin's purpose is to remind the person carrying it that now is the only moment we have. It reminds its owner that we don't have forever. It reminds me that every single moment counts and that I shouldn't waste it. I could be gone in a blink. It also means that if you don't like something in your life, change it. We have the power to make decisions. We can change our direction in an instant. Don't wait.

Martin Luther King Jr. asked, "What are you doing for others?" If that question is hard to answer, you have the power to change it. You can change the answer to that question in any given moment. If you don't think you are giving back enough, change it—right now. This moment is all we have. Do what you need to do to be the best person you can be. Don't put it off. Don't say next week. Don't wait for New Year's Day. There are millions in this world who didn't make it to last year's New Year's Eve. *Memento mori*. Live your best possible life, and start today. Remember that it doesn't have to be this big, huge thing. Small changes matter. Start serving others today. Goethe is often quoted as saying (though that has recently been debated), "Whatever you can do or dream you can, begin it; Boldness has genius, power and magic in it." So often I think we put things off because the change we want to make seems so huge. For me, that's all the more reason to start small. Volunteer to work at a local soup kitchen. Start by saying to yourself that you will commit to doing it just one time. If you like it, you will go back, maybe once a month. See what happens.

Dave is one of the guys who has been helping in the park for years. He told me once, "You know, if the first day you said to me that you needed someone to come down to the park a few days a week for years, I never would have come even once." Dave started with just one lunch break and found he wanted to come back. "Next thing I know, I've been in the game for years," he said. Start small. See where it goes.

A number of our people, such as Jim and Kelly, are down in the park every week. Some, like Dave, are there multiple times a week. Hell, one of our other Jims is down there almost every damn day with Susan and Steve. Some of these folks don't even come to Monday nights. But make no mistake: feeding those guys in the park *is* their church, and when people's time in the park lengthens, acts of mercy become something more. People start to see beyond the presenting issue of hunger and cold and start knowing people and their stories. When they know their stories, they want to see them change. It is here that justice grows. When you go beyond helping struggling people to asking *why* they struggle, then you're looking at issues of justice.

Beyond Compassion

The idea of justice goes beyond handing someone a PB&J, some chips, and a bottle of water and telling them to have a nice day. That is an act of mercy and compassion. That is valuable too, and I honestly think it can be the gateway drug for getting more involved in service and helping others. (Few things are easier than handing someone a bag of food.) Mercy and compassion are needed now in our country and our world more than ever.

But it can't stop there.

There is an old story about a group of people who lived along a river. It was a thriving, happy community. Things were going well for them. They cared for each other, everyone had enough, and the entire village had a heart for compassion.

One day, one of the people standing along the riverbank noticed something floating in the water. As they looked close, they noticed it was a little baby. Without thinking twice, the person jumped in the water, rescued the baby, and brought it to shore. The villagers gathered around the baby and realized immediately that they must raise this child. They took the child in and gave the child clean clothes, food, and warmth. The baby thrived.

It wasn't long after this that others on the riverbank noticed another child floating in the river. Again, they scooped the child up, took the child in, and saved the child from harm. The villagers really didn't know any other way. Their hearts were full of love and compassion.

This continued for a number of months, so they set up watch patrols to be on the lookout for babies in the river. People would see a baby, rescue the baby, start to raise the baby, and show the baby love and compassion.

Finally one day, after a particularly harrowing rescue, one of the villagers suddenly stood up and started walking along the river and out of the camp without saying a word. People called out to him, but he kept walking. Finally, someone ran after him, grabbed him by the shoulder, and spun him around. "Where are you going?" he said. "We need you in the village. You are one of the best at spotting the children in the water and saving their lives. What could you be going to do that is more important than that?"

The man looked at him with compassion and a determined gaze. "I'm going to find out who keeps throwing babies in the river."

The hard, drawn-out work of justice is not only about caring for those who need it, but also looking at the systems that helped contribute to getting them in that situation in the first place. Helping the homeless *is* giving them food and water and dignity. It is *also* asking why the hell it is that so many people can't afford to live indoors. It is asking what happens to a neighborhood when that neighborhood becomes cool. (Rents go up and often the poorest people who lived there up to that point can't afford their own neighborhood anymore.) It's asking why people can work full-time and *still* not afford their own apartment. (Of the people who live in shelters in Denver, 30 to 40 percent actually have jobs.) What are the systems and practices that contribute to people living on the streets in our country? These are the hard, ugly questions that social justice asks.

Often people want to jump immediately to drugs and drinking as the reason people are homeless. There is no question that for some that plays a role. But we are turning a blind eye if we think that is the only reason people are on the street. I think a lot of people like that to be the answer—because then they can say it is the person's own fault, making it much easier not to help them. But it's just not that simple. As of this writing, we have the highest number of homeless living on the streets in this country since the great recession of 2007–2009. That is messed up. We are one of the wealthiest countries in the world. We have to look at systemic issues and recognize that the deck is stacked against those on the bottom.

I attend a vigil on the longest night of the year that is a memorial for those who have died on the streets of Denver in the previous year. This year, 232 names were read. Those are the names we know; more die anonymously. It was the longest list that has ever been read since the memorial was started more than twenty-five years ago. Between 30 and 40 percent of those people died from drug- and alcohol-related reasons. That's horrible. It also means that more than half did not. They died of exposure to cold, or heat, or lack of health care, and other reasons that had nothing to do with drugs and booze.

Helping others means that we have to go beyond Band-Aids and look at what cuts people down in the first place. And it's not just the homeless who face these issues of injustice. Immigrants in our country have their backs against the wall as well. They have to endure an insane citizenship process, having to learn a completely different language, many times not knowing a soul, and horrific racism from what feels like an ever growing number of people. Global warming is another issue of justice, as not just our ecosystem but the people in it suffer due to rising temperatures, rising sea levels, failing crops, and seasons shortening and lengthening. Justice also means finding a way to right the wrongs that we have inflicted on indigenous people in our nation for far too long. Justice means fighting for all children to grow up in safe, healthy environments and fighting for them each to have a quality education regardless of family income.

These are the things that matter to our community at AfterHours. Monday gatherings are great. We gather together so that we have a sense of community, so that we know we aren't alone, so that we feel that together we can move forward just one more damn day. But even with all that, it is the service of helping others who are less fortunate that is the glue that holds us together. This glue starts to act as a bond to justice, realizing that mercy, ministry, and compassion are not completely separate from social justice. They are two sides to the same coin. I can say, almost without fail, that the social justice advocates who stick with it, who don't get burned out, and who play the long game are people who have looked into the eyes of those they are advocating for and cried tears for those they have known personally who have no more tears left to shed.

Small Acts, Big Day

Christmas in the Park is our gateway drug to social justice. One day in December has proved this year after year. And it began with a simple premise: Make Christmas suck less.

Not that Christmas sucks. For the vast majority of people, Christmas is amazing. We are with family, visiting their homes or welcoming them into ours. There is more food than we know what to do with, and more often than not, enough booze to host a standard tailgater. We are almost always surrounded by either family or people we like (both, if we are lucky). Usually we get gifts, and sometimes they are even good. On top of that, if your life has any kind of a Christian bent, you get the birth of your savior! All in all, it's not a bad way to spend the day.

Unless you are homeless. Then it sucks. There is usually no family around, no warm house with lots of food, and certainly not tailgate portions of liquor. Gifts are nowhere to be seen, never mind if they are good. And to top it off, if you do have a religious leaning in your life, many times you are struggling hard to figure out what you did to piss God off so much that he made you homeless.

About nine years ago, a group of about eight of us thought, "Man, it's gotta suck to be homeless on Christmas Day." (And yes, we were well aware that it ain't a knee-slapper the other 364 days of the year.) We thought about things we could do to change that.

It was out of this that Christmas in the Park was born.

Fast-forward nine years later. Over 700 of our friends without homes showed up and got just about anything you could think of under the sun, short of a new car and a place to live. We gave away over 500 winter coats and more than 700 sleeping bags. With two grills, we grilled more than 1,200 cheeseburgers in just over three hours—that is more than 400 burgers *an hour*. Your local McDonald's isn't knockin' out that kind of flow.

More than 500 volunteers came together and brought whatever they had. Some brought egg salad sandwiches, toothbrushes, toothpaste, hand warmers (it was twenty-six degrees this Christmas—they went fast). There was men's underwear and socks and gloves and hats and scarves and boots. There were over 200 rolls of duct tape and more tarps than I could count. There were piles and piles of jeans and hundreds and hundreds of backpacks. There was hot chocolate and coffee and candy and carolers. Hell, even Santa made an appearance.

There was Communion too—lots and lots of Communion (although the grape juice almost froze—kind of a blood of Christ slushee).

We even had a port-a-potty. From a distance, it really did look like a *huge* tailgate party. And it kinda was. It was a tailgate party for the little baby Jesus.

All three of our local TV networks came out, and the *Denver Post* did a really nice piece on us. All in all, it was a great day.

I don't say this to pat ourselves on the back. We had a lot of snafus, like we do every year: walkie-talkies that are useless, people in lines who sometimes push and shove, stuff that runs out, and—this happens every year—someone who comes late and doesn't get anything.

The point here isn't how much we got right, or even how much we got wrong. It's that we tried. We showed up.

We started small and kept at it. And we grew and grew and grew. Now we have flags designating "shopping areas," and yellow reflective vests, and megaphones, and did I mention the port-a-potties? When you bring your own toilet, it's a serious party!

I want to be clear: this is not an event *for* the homeless; it is an event *with* the homeless. This event doesn't just make Christmas a little better for those standing in line waiting for a subzero sleeping bag. It changes the people giving away the sleeping bags too—and the hot chocolate, and the egg salad sandwiches, and the duct tape, and the fresh grilled cheeseburgers.

It's helping all of us. We are all broken. We just need fixing in different ways.

It reminds me of what Christmas is, and what it isn't. It reminds me that as Mike Slaughter has pointed out, Christmas is not *your* birthday. It is *Jesus'* birthday, and what Jesus wants for a present—that day and every day—is for us to love each other like he loved us.

We have gotten this holiday flipped 180 degrees since its inception. It's not about what you grab under the tree and rip open. It's about what's in your hands that you then give away.

Christmas in the Park reminds us what the meaning of Christmas is. It reminds us of the spirit of giving. It reminds us that we are not alone. It reminds us that we are wired to be in community *and* that we are wired to help. It is born into our DNA.

And it is so easy to forget. This year we had some additional reminders. We had the local business community. We had local bars putting out bins to collect clothes in the weeks leading up to the event. We had truck rental companies giving us free trucks to take the coats and sleeping bags downtown. We had pubs loan us trash cans to distribute throughout the park. We had a tavern completely underwrite our entire Christmas fund-raiser so that we could put all our money back into what we do best. Coffee and hot cocoa were donated, along with thousands of dollars' worth of winter coats and gear from Patagonia.

What all this tells me is that people are hungry to do good. We are hungry to make a difference. We are hungry to help the hungry. We are starving to change the world for the better. All we have to do is provide the vehicle. I am convinced that after nine years, this event doesn't need me—and that's a good thing. It is now running smoothly enough that if I were to get hit by a bus tomorrow, Christmas in the Park would still be going strong year after year.

We don't have to drag people. People are waiting. As proof, we know of at least two other cities (Colorado Springs and San Diego) that have started their own giveaways on Christmas Day. We have watched it grow. Now we are watching it spread.

Folks, Christmas in the Park can take place in *any* city, big or small. You can help make it happen. If you want to connect to something bigger and you can't find it, make it.

Seeing people on both sides of the grill with tears in their eyes? Money can't buy that.

One woman said, "I rarely if ever see tears in my husband's eyes. Today after helping out, I saw his eyes well up."

I saw people take it upon themselves to just pick up trash. That was their whole gig. Every time I saw Chris or Mandy, they were either hauling trash away or they were filling a trash bag with things people left behind. It takes a special kind of humility to spend most of your time with the homeless picking up their trash. And make no mistake: they were picking up an equal amount of trash from the volunteers; 1,200 people can leave a lot behind. When we left, the park was cleaner than when we got there.

This year we tried something new. We found people to volunteer to go through the line with anyone who might need extra assistance. We told people that if they wanted to and felt comfortable, they could go to a designated spot and have a concierge walk with them through the line and help them "shop." To sit back and watch how kindly and compassionately these volunteers walked the line with folks and helped them shop with a bit more ease and a bit more dignity restored my faith—again.

Get out into your community. Find your peeps. Find a way to serve. Your life will be changed. I promise.

Martin Luther King Jr. was such an amazing orator. I have been lucky enough to stand in the pulpit of his church in Montgomery and in the pulpit of Central United Methodist Church in Detroit where he delivered an earlier version of his "I Have a Dream" speech on June 23, 1963. My mom was pregnant with me then. Both times I stood in those pulpits years later, it gave me chills.

Dr. King understood the power of service. He understood how it changed lives from the inside out. He said this: "Everybody can be great . . . because anybody can serve. You don't have to have a college degree to serve. You don't have to make your subject and verb agree to serve. You only need a heart full of grace. A soul generated by love."[4]

King also said that darkness cannot drive out darkness. Only light can do that.

On Christmas Day 2017 in downtown Denver, darkness didn't stand a chance. We kicked its ass.

FOR HEATHENS' EYES ONLY

Vesper

According to James Bond in *Casino Royale*, chapter 7, the recipe for the vesper is as follows: "Three measures of Gordon's, one of vodka, half a measure of Kina Lillet. Shake it very well until it's ice-cold, then add a large thin slice of lemon peel."

It's actually a pretty easy recipe to follow. As long as you keep the proportions right, it turns out pretty good: three parts gin, one part vodka, half a part Lillet.

Remember to make sure it's really, really cold—like Detroit-in-the-middle-of-February cold.

And, of course, for God's sake, if you want to make it like JB likes 'em, make sure you shake it and don't stir it. (This flies in the face of most bartender protocol, which tells you to stir . . . but don't be an ass. We don't need drink police. Drinking should be fun.)

Chapter Three

Love Kindness:
Don't Be an Asshat

THE SPIRITUALITY OF . . . HORSES

Claire McNulty-Drewes is a gentle soul with an easy laugh. She wasn't raised in the church, but she became a Methodist pastor. As a result, I get the sense she thinks that all the denominational crap is silly and that she really just wants to love God and people. She is not scared off by bawdy language, and she can do a tequila shot with the best of them. She has a huge, contagious laugh that is impossible not to love. She is my kind of person. And while she says she does indeed love God and love people, it was horses that changed her life.

Claire has been around horses since she was a child. She competed on horses and knows them, from feeding them to riding them and everything in between. And something about their power combined with their gentle nature made Claire know they had to be a part of her life.

She is drawn to the misunderstood and the troublemakers—the horses that others didn't have time for, those who struggle with trust. Those are the ones she wants to put her time and energy into.

From a young age, she remembers being connected to God through her experiences with horses. She told me, "I remember being on the back of a horse going at full gallop through a field and thinking, 'This must be what heaven is like.'" You have to communicate with horses differently; you can't pull around a 2,000-pound animal. You have to have a way of connecting without words. In many ways, the same can be said of the universe or the divine. Communicating goes beyond words. It is a feeling you get.

She told me that being around horses helped her be in better touch not only with herself but with the people around her. "My trainer would say to me, 'Stop nagging. You're nagging the horse.' I realized that not only was this useful with the horse, but it was useful with my husband or kids."

About a month ago, I was talking with a clergy buddy of mine, and we were complaining about the church. (Don't be fooled; we bitch and moan just like people in any other job.)

After much complaining about church politics, mean parishioners, and horrible committee gatherings where a lot of "real" decisions are actually made in the "parking lot meetings" that take place after the actual meetings, she finally turned to me and said, "Can people just not be dicks? Isn't that the gospel in a nutshell?" I had to agree.

The church and its employees have gotten so good at "speaking the truth in love" and "blessing their heart" before they say some hateful shit that we have forgotten the basic tenets of just being kind.

We have to face the fact that Christians have a terrible reputation—not all, but many. We want to think we are known for our hospitals and universities and soup kitchens, but a lot of that was built a *long time ago*. Are we *still* riding on that? When it comes to the day to day, we have to own the fact that, more often than not, the way Christians interact with others is no better than the way anyone else interacts with others. Pile on top of that arrogance, condescension, and a lack of humility, and we are not going to win the "most likable" award at our job or at our neighborhood block party anytime soon.

I can already hear some of my fellow Christians: "I'm not here to be liked. I am here to speak the truth to power and to afflict the comfortable." Sigh. While I don't disagree with this sentiment, so often these phrases are coming out of some of the most angry, mean-spirited people I know. I think they sometimes use these phrases just so that can say some hurtful shit but cloak it in "Christian love." And to be clear, in my experience, it is not just the far-right Christians being so hurtful, and rarely if ever is it marginalized people, who often times have every right to be angry. (People actually *on* the margins of society have shown this straight, able-bodied, struggling-to-be-a-good-ally, white boy *way* more grace than I deserve.) Liberal Christians can be stunningly cutting and cruel, all in the name of "holiness." It can sometimes feel like the Justice Olympics: "No, I'm more outraged!" "No, I care more!" Pleeeease.

I know that there is such a thing as righteous anger, and I know—since I exemplify the previously mentioned quadfecta of privilege (white, male, straight, able-bodied) —that I am not qualified to question others' righteous anger. On almost every metric, I have had it easy. I have zero right to comment on any marginalized group's anger. I have been surprised, though, by a number of allies on the liberal side who at times become almost blind with anger, more so than the marginalized groups themselves.

How's that working out for us? Is the anger bringing more love into the situation? I know very few people who have been shamed or hurt or humiliated into thinking differently. Such pressure might change their actions; it might also drive them not to mention aloud what they really think in front of us again. But how do we change their minds and hearts? Only love will change those. Shaming others rarely works, whether it is with your dog, your kids, or your enemies. Compassion and love, on the other hand, often have a pretty good success rate. Ask Mandela, Tutu, or King.

Whether the preacher is condemning gay folks or condemning folks who condemn gay folks, negative, shame-filled preaching drives a lot of people away from the church. It may well be what drove you out of the church.

I posted a question on Facebook awhile back. I do this a lot. Sometimes they get traction, sometimes people just shake their collective heads and say, "What a sad, sad little man."

This one got some traction—more than eighty-five comments: What is the purpose of preaching?

No one who commented claimed that the purpose of preaching was to condemn sinners or arouse people's anger (the righteous or unrighteous kind). But neither did they say much about the way people who profess to follow Jesus should live.

Only one response mentioned Jesus.

We as the church (and really I mean preachers) have to show the connection between Jesus and kindness, Jesus and grace, and Jesus and compassion. Richard Rohr has said it is crucial to remember that Jesus didn't have a hard time with sinners—he had a hard time with people who didn't think they were sinners.[1]

Jesus was the model for compassion, kindness, and being nonjudgmental, which makes me wonder why the church and preachers have a history of struggling with all three. Shaming so often leads the day, with judgment coming in a close second. This to me is the antithesis of Jesus' teachings.

I confess that I can get the heebie-jeebies if I hear the "Jeeeeeesus" talk too much (add one heebie-jeebie for every "e" in Jesus). Having said that, I do think at the very least that we have to own the fact that this *is* the dude Christians say they are trying to follow.

Instead, it seems like we have confused preaching with TED Talks and sermons for motivational speeches. The end goal can't be just to inspire, or to teach, or to offer hope, or to proclaim, or to untangle, or to dream, or to provide insight, or to offer vision. (These were all answers to my question given on the Facebook thread.) All of those are good and important. But they aren't the purpose of preaching.

It's funny that people often think we at AfterHours are so radical because we meet in bars, that we are so liberal because we might have a beer in front of us while we gather.

One thing we are not, however, is afraid to use the word *Jesus*. We mention him every week. For me the reason is simple: we are called to be like him. We are called to learn about Jesus for the purpose of living like he lived.

Not *hearing* how he lived.

Not *studying* how he lived.

Not *being a fan* of how he lived.

Living like he lived.

My main job when I am preaching is to challenge and inspire the folks who are listening to live like Jesus. That's it. That's the whole gig! And the real kicker is that many of the people who live like Jesus the best at AfterHours still have their jury out on whether they want to formally "follow" him or not. Some of the best Jesus followers I know are atheists! I would love to say that this is because of my awesome three-point sermons, but that simply ain't the case. Hell, at one of our locations, I don't even lead the conversation; they wrestle at their tables with a question I throw out there. (More times than not they will ask me my thoughts on the question later, one on one, but I think that is deeper and more meaningful anyway.) When I do kick off the discussion, it's much more like jazz than symphony music. It has more dialogue and is more free-flowing. It is more Muddy Waters and nothing like Bach. My whole goal is to bring people back to trying to live like Jesus. Because that is what a disciple is: someone who *follows* and *lives like* the teacher.

Preaching should challenge and inspire anyone listening to live like Jesus. I believe it is a call to action. The Gospel of John talks about the Word becoming flesh. I think that is kick-ass. The Word becomes Jesus. When we do it right, our words can move people to become more like Jesus—to take flesh-and-blood action to make this world a better place.

If the words spoken in church don't change who people are at a core level, if they don't change the way people function and interact with the world, and if they don't make us want to put more love into it by living our life like Jesus lived his, then we preachers have failed.

St. Francis is famous for his instruction, "Preach the gospel at all times. If necessary, use words." The church has got to start preaching the gospel again—preferably with its mouth shut.

As for me, I preach loudest when I'm serving folks on the street in Denver—usually with my mouth shut.

We had an awful winter day once, and a team of us was feeding folks in the park. It was the kind of day when the wind was blowing the snow sideways, and honestly, none of us wanted to be there. (Ask any of the folks who come down to the park on a weekly basis. There are days when you just aren't feelin' it.)

I said what I always say when I offer someone Communion: "This is a reminder of how much God loves you." As I said these words to Eddie, one of our regulars, he replied without missing a beat: "You guys are a reminder of how much God loves me."

That stopped me in my tracks. I flashed back to the words of the Communion liturgy: "Pour out your Holy Spirit on us gathered here, and on these gifts of bread and wine. Make them be for us the body and blood of Christ, so that we may be for the world the body of Christ."

We take God in so that we can take God out—into the world. We are the sacrament. We are to be like Jesus. We are words made flesh, if we choose—if we choose to get out there and live like him. Not just agree with him. As the little ditty says, they will know we are Christians by our love.

And to paraphrase St. Francis, we need to shut up and preach.

Learn Their Story

Now that I am north of fifty, I have found that I am less interested in how others think and act and more interested in their stories. What was it in their stories that *got* them to think and act as they do? I've found that when I know their stories better and better, their actions often don't seem as unexplainable, and it's easier to treat them with kindness. I hear a lot of stories about homelessness too. I hear how they got there. When you hear the events that led up to people becoming homeless, your perception of them changes. I have realized that very few people

are black-and-white. We are a spectrum of gray. This is
not to give bad behavior a pass. But it is to say that compassion grows when you hear someone's story.

Consider Rob's story. Rob is absolutely a "good-
hearted heathen." He lives a . . . full life, shall we say.
He has a good time. He calls bullshit when he sees it.
He is a regular at AfterHours but sometimes leaves after
we make the sandwiches. Sometimes he comes after the
sandwiches are made and hangs around. He has lived a
hard life out in the world, and he goes to his own tune,
travels his own path. And we love him just as he is. Rob
kind of reminds me of the "hooker with a heart of gold"
type. He is cool in all the right ways, and you get the
sense that his good looks and charm, talent, and humor
might make him more "rogue" than "saint." Turns out,
that's not the case. He's not big on dogma, but he is big
on leading with love and leaving the rest of the crap by
the roadside.

He has gotten deeply involved with Helping Hands,
an organization that works to relieve human suffering all
over the globe. And he's the one who reached out to Patagonia and got them to donate those thousands of dollars'
worth of jackets and gear for Christmas in the Park. He
did this all on his own. One day I just got a text that said,
"I need AfterHours' tax-exempt number." Next thing I
know, we got tons of shit to give to the homeless that I
had nothing to do with.

There is a great quote by Wes Angelozzi: "Go and
love someone exactly as they are. And watch how quickly
they transform into the greatest, truest version of themselves. When one feels seen and appreciated in their own
essence, one is instantly empowered."[2]

I would take a bunch of Robs over those who might
know the Bible inside out but live their lives with hurtful

words and actions. Rob's not that guy. He might say, "I think you're full of shit and here's why . . . ," but I would take that any day over the alternative.

Rob lives his life by leading with love and compassion. He still gets pissed, still gets hungover, and still probably does some things that might not land him in everyone's angel category. But he is real and authentic and a straight shooter, and you always know what you are getting with him.

I think Jesus was a lot like that too. Rob is exactly the type of person I had hoped would find AfterHours.

Plato has often been credited with this quote: "Be kind to everyone, for everyone is fighting a hard battle." Whoever said it, the sentiment is life-changing. When we realize that what we see of people's lives is just the tip of the iceberg, we realize that we simply can't be so quick to judge. Often people seem like less of an ass once you understand what they are going through.

I will grant you, this is hard as hell. There are, quite honestly, some people I don't want to "get"—people I don't want to "understand." It is much easier (and in some ways, more fun) just to hate them where they're at! It's easy to watch someone for a bit, think I've got them figured out, and then call them out, shame them, and say my piece—all the while cloaking it as "speaking the truth in love." Understanding others takes more time, more energy, and more compassion. It's just flat-out harder.

Oh well. Tough shit. That's what we are called to do—to love one another.

When we think back to Jesus, the dude was *nailed to a cross!* He had just been tortured within an inch of his life and now was hanging on a cross, nailed in place by metal spikes driven through his hands and feet. But what did he say? "Father, forgive them; for they do not know what they are doing."

Seriously? If anyone had the right to be pissed, it was Jesus while he was hanging on a tree waiting to die. But he asks God to forgive the very people who are torturing him. That makes me think a little differently about those I have viewed as enemies or attackers.

Exercising compassion and understanding the other person's story change us at a core level—and make us less of a tool. And couldn't we all be tools a little less?

Called to the Crossroads

Frederick Buechner once said, "The place God calls you to is the place where your deep gladness and the world's deep hunger meet."[3] We're pretty good at finding our own gladness (though not necessarily the "deep" kind), but seeing the world's hunger is a lot harder. It requires looking beyond ourselves to others. It requires compassion.

Having started in stand-up back in the late 1980s, I can tell you that there are few professions that scream "Look at me!" more than comedy. In fact, the entire career is made up of just that: you, all alone, standing on the stage, saying words that you believe are witty and interesting enough to have everyone else in the room stop talking and just listen to you. You have to think very highly of yourself to even believe you can attempt it.

I was an entertainer and performer for nearly thirty years. My first paying gig was in 1985 at the Cedar Point amusement park in Sandusky, Ohio. I did a fifteen-minute one-man show there in a thousand-seat theater forty-two times a week, and every show was packed. That means 42,000 people a week watched me perform. Now, they didn't come to see *me* perform. They came to see the IMAX show that immediately followed me, and I was what they had to put up with for the fifteen minutes prior to the lights going down. I got a lot of experience and made $210 every week! (For those of you who are doing the math in your head, I can help you out—it was five bucks a show. But, hey, I was in show biz!)

In 1987, I packed up my car and headed to L.A. with the goal of taking over *The Tonight Show*. Even though I had to pick up some bartending gigs in the beginning, I also started working right away. I did audience warm-ups for a number of shows, signed a contract to write for Jay Leno, and was the house emcee at the Improv on Melrose in Hollywood. (I split the emcee duty with another fellow named Judd Apatow, who went on to direct some of the biggest comedies in Hollywood, including *The 40-Year-Old Virgin* and *Trainwreck*. He doesn't return my calls.)

I was pretty happy with the work I was getting, but I was barely making ends meet. Add to that the L.A. riots and the Northridge earthquake, which had my wife and I sleeping in our car for a couple of nights, and we decided to pack it in.

We moved to Orlando, where I became an entertainment manager at a nightclub and continued performing all over the country, and we were "fine." I just had this nagging sense that I was wasting my life—again. My wife, Laura, wanted to go back to church, which she really hadn't done our whole time in L.A. So we found a church with a good preacher and an excellent choir, and suddenly we were back to being churchgoers.

One day I was meeting with our pastor, Bill Barnes, to discuss my feelings of malaise. What I was doing was OK, but there was a sense that I was born for something more. "You ever think about ministry?" Bill said to me as

I did a spit take. "Bill," I said, "I curse like a sailor, I like brown liquor, and I look at pretty girls when they go by. I am *not* cut out for ministry." I figured that was the end of the discussion.

What Bill said next changed my life. "Maybe you're just the guy. Maybe you can be yourself and show people that ministers are struggling along just like everyone else."

It took seven years for me to actually follow up on Bill's suggestion, but ultimately we moved to Denver so I could go to seminary. Even after finishing seminary and getting placed in St. Andrew United Methodist Church, a large suburban church outside of Denver, I knew I wasn't a perfect fit. I fit the criteria: straight, white, middle-aged male with a pretty wife and cute kid, but I kept feeling this pull to be with folks who lived on the street.

I wish I had a cool story to explain the root of my connection to the homeless, but I don't. I had volunteered with homeless groups before, but never on a consistent basis. I had an uncle who was homeless, but we had met only a couple of times. The truth is, I think sometimes God and/or the universe throws you a curve. I wonder if God said, "What have you always admired? Power, fame, money, approval, nice clothes, a cool house, a good job you love? Yeah, well, no. I am going to have some people tug at your heart who have none of those things. And believe it or not, you are going to fall in love with them."

You don't always see love coming.

We started AfterHours out of St. Andrew and immediately started making PB&Js in the worship service to take down to feed the homeless one day a week. Seven years later, AfterHours is its own church; we partner with other churches and law firms and moms' groups, and we feed a hundred people a day, 365 days a year. It didn't happen overnight, which I try to make clear to other churches just starting out. It was gradual; it happened almost without us seeing it.

Buechner was right. It is about finding the crossroads. I *loved* entertaining and doing comedy. It was a deep gladness—but I don't know if it was the world's deep hunger. With my current work, I am creating joy in a different way *and* meeting a deep hunger (fingers crossed).

Buechner's quote makes a great compass for finding your most meaningful place in the world. Chances are, you know what makes you truly happy (at least, I hope you do). Discovering your passion can bring you to life—it can get you out of the tomb that often is your current life. It can feel like cold water splashing against your face. That intersection of personal passion and the communal good can change your world forever. Do the two meet for you now? Could they meet even more precisely? Keep asking, "Is this the best place for my gladness and the world's needs to meet?"

This search for the crossroads is not easy work. It can often feel like the universe is putting up roadblocks. It can feel like we are sometimes banging our heads against the wall. But the alternative sucks a lot worse. Thoreau was right when he said that most people "lead lives of quiet desperation." This desperation can vanish when you find that call. When that happens, kindness and compassion magically appear more often in your life on a day-to-day basis, and by God, you want to pass it on! The kindness and compassion that you pass on come from overflow. I have seen it so many times. It is magical, and it feels like you are watching a miracle.

To go about our days doing the same thing day after day, week after week, year after year and getting little to no satisfaction from it breaks God's heart. I truly believe that. As I have said before, I am not big on quoting Bible passages. I think it makes one sound like a pretentious asshat. So let me do it now. (Don't worry; I only know a couple.) John 10:10 says that God's wish for us is abundant life. Now that doesn't mean there won't be hurts and that we won't get knocked on our ass every now and then. But I think it does mean that God wants for us a life that is full and rich and meaningful. I think God wants you to go out there and get it, to move forward in a way that, at the end of the day, you know you have impacted the world in a way that only you can—that you have made this place just a little bit better and, God forbid, actually enjoyed it!

And it doesn't have to be just your "work." Sometimes when you find the activity that lights you up, you become a better person all around—better able to feel others' hurts and see their needs. Look for the thing that fills you so that you'll have something to give the world.

Curtis Brown is someone who has found his "thing." Curtis has been a friend and colleague for about ten years. I consider Curtis like Rain Man when it comes to church. He knows things. But the thing that really helps him connect to something larger than himself is backpacking. Now I am not a backpacker. There's nothing about me even remotely that screams backpacking. Hell, it doesn't even whisper backpacking. My idea of roughing it is staying at a hotel without room service and a lobby bar. But everybody swings on their own vine.

At first I was a bit skeptical of Curtis's "the trees, the sky, and the moon" spirituality. I mean, everybody and their brother says they connect to God through nature. Honestly, what more is there to say? But backpacking is in Curtis's blood. He has been backpacking all his life, since he was little. Pitching a tent for him comes as simple as breathing. When he lived in Spain, he hiked with his Boy Scout troop over the Pyrenees mountains every year—yes, every year. I had to look at a map. Apparently, the Pyrenees are the mountain range that separates Spain from France. Who knew? (Granted, maybe a lot of you. Don't gloat.) He said, "I really liked it. There is something about putting everything you need on your back and stepping away from your car."

He used phrases like "your sleeping bag system." There's a system? I just thought you climb in and zip it up. Apparently, I was doing this all wrong.

Regardless of the fact that every ten minutes he had to explain to me what a "shakedown hike" was or a "glacier cirque," Curtis's love for backpacking was evident, and it was far more than a delight in gear and terminology. He mentioned a field of theology called "natural theology," what we know about God through the study of nature, and how he tries to spend his birthday each year out in the wilderness. He also mentioned running into a guy hiking in only a gold thong and hiking boots. He called him "mostly naked guy," and I'm not sure where he was hiking. Vegas? Key West? Carnival in Rio? He might have told me, but I have been trying to forget it. It will haunt me for a while. He also talked about the power of Oreos to instigate human connection (note to self).

He told me that the most significant moment on his spiritual journey happened outside. He remembers looking around and thinking, "This world is *amazing!*" He believes that being on the trail is "a stripping away of the things that keep me separated from the awesomeness of God."

The thing is, the things that keep us separated from God can also keep us separated from one another—self-centeredness, pride, judgment. Curtis told me about a saying they have in the backpacking world: "Hike your own hike. Nobody is going to take the journey the same way, and whatever it is that is feeding your spirit is probably exactly what you should be doing."

I think this advice goes beyond hiking. We are all called to "hike our own hike." I think one of the problems of the traditional church is a tendency to make us feel like there is a "right way to 'do God'"—that there is only one hike. This irritates the hell out of me, and I know it drives a lot of non-Christians crazy.

We are all born in the image of God, and no two of us look alike (even the Olsen twins). We are all, as a buddy of mine says, "unique little snowflakes." What makes us think that the way we connect to God would be cookie-cutter? For some people, like Curtis, it's backpacks and sleeping-bag systems and Oreos (and seeing an occasional almost naked guy in a thong). That isn't going to work for everyone. I would even venture to say it isn't going to work for most people. And that's OK.

Go out and find that thing and make it yours—that thing that only you can do, that thing that benefits the world and brings you fulfillment and joy. Every day won't be a day at the circus. Some days will blow. But the blow-to-joy ratio shouldn't be very high. Every job is going to have "those days." But if the crappy days start to outnumber the good ones, it's time to do some rethinking.

We are not promised joy. We are not promised contentment. We are not promised satisfaction. I think all those things are truly God's desire for us, but we have to do our part.

I think God works in partnership with us. As my mom used to say, "God feeds the birds, but he doesn't throw food into the nest." When we make the effort, we will often find all kinds of doors starting to open. As Paulo Coelho wrote in *The Alchemist*, "When you want something, all the universe conspires in helping you achieve it." God *wants* us to have an abundant life!

This may sound selfish or even like I'm veering into prosperity preaching, but joy can change the world. When we don't feel connected to something bigger, something that inspires us, it's easier to act like an ass. We feel stuck and out of sorts, and as a result, we aren't always the greatest people to be around. I know that's been true with me.

Joy *always* leads to kindness. When we are firing on all cylinders, we want others to as well. When we partner with God, all boats rise.

FOR HEATHENS' EYES ONLY

Vieux Carre

3/4 oz. rye whiskey
3/4 oz. cognac
3/4 oz. sweet vermouth
1 bar spoon Benedictine
2 dashes Peychaud's bitters
2 dashes Angostura bitters

Dump everything into a mixing glass and fill with ice. Stir. Strain into an ice-filled old-fashioned glass and garnish. (Some say cherry. I say lemon—and I'm not the only one.)

This drink is a pain in the ass to make. Not every bar has Peychaud's bitters, and even fewer these days have Benedictine, but if you go into a joint that looks like they know their way around a fancy drink, order it. I guarantee the bartender will smile.

Chapter Four

Walk Humbly, with Your Head Held High

THE SPIRITUALITY OF . . . FLY FISHING

"Everybody in Old Testament fly-fishes."

This was not what I expected Andy Blackum to say when I asked him how he got into fly-fishing. I got my master of divinity degree in 2007, and while I know I have forgotten a lot of things from my Hebrew Bible class, I am relatively certain that I would remember if Ishmael or Joshua were casting into the River Jordan. (I will grant you that Moses was known to have a rod in his hand, but I always read that differently.)

Turns out that what Andy was referring to was Old Testament scholars. Andy is married to Katherine Turpin, one of my seminary professors, and as a result, he comes into contact with a number of religious educators. Professors Gene Tucker, Mark George, David Petersen, among others, all fly-fish. I asked him what he thought the correlation was for Hebrew Bible scholars between their profession and fly-fishing. He thinks it has to do with the appreciation of the artistry involved (tying the knots, perfecting your cast, and so forth) and that most Hebrew Bible scholars see the same beauty in the language of the Old Testament and the artistry of the authors in crafting that historic text.

71

While some would see fishing as a cruel sport, Andy, along with many others, practices catch and release, which doesn't kill the fish. In fact, studies have shown that when handled carefully, the fish go on to thrive. He did acknowledge that "it's an imposition on the fish." This made me laugh—as if the fish had other plans down the river and this threw off his whole schedule. All in all, it is a beautiful and (relatively) cruelty-free sport.

When I asked him why fly-fishing was a spiritual experience for him, he told me that one of the biggest things was patience, both in a proper cast (he talked about having to wait in the middle of the cast while "loading the rod") and in waiting for the fish to bite. "You can't make that fish 'do' anything," he said. For him it is a calming process. It tames anxiety.

He also said it wasn't about actually catching fish. For Andy, fly-fishing provides an outlet to connect with other men. He has gone on fishing trips for three days and had a great time in spite of the fact they didn't catch any fish.

When I asked him about traditional church, he cut right to the chase. "I don't have a lot of use for the institutional church. I'll sit through it, but I'm just not completely there. Mentally? I'm on the water."

Because when he's on the water, he is practicing patience, taming anxiety, and connecting with other people. Andy told me, "Fly-fishing is a continual exercise in hope."

There are a lot worse ways to spend an afternoon.

It is 6:30 in the morning. I had to get up at 5:30, so right off the bat, I am out of my element and kinda pissed.

I drive to the church and get out. I am both looking forward to this and nervous. The thing is, I'm not going to worship. I'm going into the church basement.

I'm going to an AA meeting.

More than once people have seen me have a drink. More than once I have stolen Frank Sinatra's line, "I don't drink a lot. I don't drink a little either." I have always enjoyed a beer, glass of wine, or a tumbler of bourbon. Nine times out of ten, I have been sensible, but I have had some occasions of being overserved. I'm not proud of those moments.

Today, though, I am coming face-to-face with people with a different history. The people in this room have had a very different experience with alcohol. They realize they don't have control and are doing the very hard work to not drink again. I will not mention anyone by name—I am aware of what the second "A" means—nor will I repeat any of the stories I hear. What happens there deserves to stay there.

The reason I am there is that one of my best friends is getting his five-year chip. He texted me and asked me to come. I was the first person he called that morning five years ago, and he wanted me to be present when he got his five-year coin. It is an honor to be there.

I do catch myself having anxiety about going. What if someone sees me there? What if they think I was there for *myself*? Am I going to be treated as an outsider? Am I even going to be allowed in the room?

I have said this before and I will say it again: I think AA meetings are the most accurate representation of what the early church gatherings were like. There is no main leader; people take turns running the meeting. There is no tithe. People donate money to cover expenses. There is listening—lots and lots of listening. There is compassion. People demonstrate a willingness to transform their lives. There is desire to help others along the way. There is, as my friend Tony mentioned earlier in the book, a cornerstone of service. (At one point, someone finishes doing a relatively mundane activity—passing out chips to people celebrating a milestone in their sobriety—and after completing the task says, "Thank you for letting me be of service." That blows me away.) There is also humility—tons of humility—and gratitude. You can feel it as soon as you walk in the room.

The room feels holy. It is sacred ground. The only calling out I hear is when people call themselves out, recalling and expressing remorse for times they were "showing off" or "being a dick." There is no fancy language, no insider lingo, no secret moves or acronyms that make me feel like I'm not in the know. It feels welcoming. I can see why, even in the midst of their struggle, people keep coming back. The room feels safe and encouraging.

AfterHours was modeled after what little I knew about AA meetings. I wanted multiple people to have a voice. I wanted people to feel safe. I wanted there to be a lack of judgment. I wanted people to feel it was OK to say what was on their mind and heart and not just throw back up the standard crap that they had heard at so many other churches whether they believed it or not. I wanted there to be no insider language of the type that keeps so many people away from the church in the first place. And I wanted people to know that no one has perfect answers and that we are all limping along together.

I realized after that one AA meeting that AfterHours needs to do a better job with humility. This is probably because *I* need to do a better job with humility. It is still a character flaw for me to shout, "Look at me!" I am better than I was but not nearly as good as I could be. I recently had someone in a clergy meeting put her arm around me and say in front of the group, "I think you need to listen a little more and talk a little less." It was really hurtful. It embarrassed me and shamed me and humiliated me, and the reason it was all those things was probably because it was true. While I would disagree with the way she did it, there was probably more than a grain of truth to it. I do like contributing to the larger discussion, and hopefully what I say will have some worth to those hearing it. Regardless, I could probably do it less.

It's a tough balance, especially when you think you have good things to share. AfterHours is proud of the work we do. We like helping change the world, and we enjoy putting more love into it. We talk about it a lot on social media and consider this our primary form of marketing. We make no bones about that. As often as possible we try to direct the attention either to those on the street or to our volunteers. Both of those groups of people are the real heroes of our story. The challenges that our homeless brothers and sisters face on a daily basis is mind-boggling, and I am pretty sure I would suck at it. Our volunteers do a stunning amount of work and are out in the park handing out food when it is blistering hot or bone-chilling cold. (Our record cold for the last seven years is eight degrees.)

We try to find the balance between sharing good news and bragging. Humility is hard to name, but we sure do know it when we *don't* see it.

Feeling Small

There are a lot of ways to find our humility. My friend Mark C. Cordes is a take-no-prisoners, tell-it-like-it-is, ministry-is-a-contact-sport kind of guy. With a bald head and a build like a linebacker, he is an intimidating force of nature. When Mark wants to get his feet wet experiencing humility, he does it literally—out on his surfboard.

That, he tells me, is where he finds his connection to something bigger. "The amount of pressure and strength that a wave can create is mind-boggling," he says. "I don't care how big a guy you are—when you are about to get crushed by a wave, you feel really, really small." The ocean reminds him of just how human and just how small he really is. He says that the ocean has a way of keeping you humble. He lives in the San Francisco Bay area and tries to get out in the ocean whenever he can.

"I haven't gotten out there as often as I want of late," he confesses. "The job keeps me running, and life has gotten busy. I need to get back to it."

Since then, Mark is recommitting to getting back into the surf. When Mark puts his mind to something, he makes it happen. He knows that the fun of surfing can make it deceiving. The ocean is a great teacher, and there are more lessons to be learned, humility being lesson number one.

Jim Francis is half of the team affectionately known simply as "the Jims." Jim Francis and Jim McKeever have been a couple for fourteen and a half years, and have been married for the last four and a half. They model servant leadership, and I can't imagine AfterHours without them. They are both on the leadership team and in the park on a weekly basis.

Jim Francis told me that he hit a spot in his forties when he realized his life was "all about Jim"—and he didn't mean the other Jim. "I was putting myself first in everything I do, and the world is bigger than just me. There was an easy turn I could make, in starting to attend AfterHours. It gave me a vehicle to step outside of the box of me." I love that language: "the box of me."

Getting out of this box has bled over into other areas of his life. "To open myself to the need of other people has made me a better person in general. My empathy for the situation other people find themselves in has made me a better manager at work, a better youth ministry leader, and a better spouse." This is the kind of humility service brings.

And you can't go back. "Today I cannot imagine being 'all about Jim' as I once was," he says. "I see how my interaction with our friends in the park brightens their days. My prayer is that giving a smile, which costs nothing, will bring a little light to the darkness that shadows so many lives."

That is a humility seen far too rarely in the world. Jim's got it figured out.

Sometimes, though, life makes it easy to feel humble. When we get too "all about us," the universe has a way of helping us out. Sometimes it can be as easy as the surroundings themselves to put you in your place.

Don's Club Tavern—also known as Don's Mixed Drinks—is a weird duck. We do AfterHours right in the middle of the bar. People are always walking up and saying, "What's going on here?" We tell them we are making sandwiches for the homeless, and often they will join right in. It's kinda awesome.

Recently a couple shooting pool asked what was going on. We told them about the sandwiches, and I could tell they were visibly moved. After a while one of them said, "So where do you get the money for this?" I told him, "You." (Someone at AfterHours says I'm the king of the soft sell.) I told him that we get donations from all over the country, that people believe in what we are doing and make donations. He reached in his wallet and handed us twenty bucks. I'm always reminded that, at its core, humanity doesn't suck.

That same night after we had made sandwiches and

I was finishing my talk, we were breaking into groups to continue the conversation in a smaller setting when two men pulled up bar stools. I introduced myself and asked them their names. They were middle-aged, white, average-looking guys. I caught them up on what we were talking about and told them that even though they missed making sandwiches, and most of my talk, they were still welcome to join our conversation. They listened intently as I explained the topic and the questions we were discussing. At this point, one of them leaned in and said to me, "Yeah, so we don't really know what AfterHours is and what you are doing here. My friend here is from Cincinnati," he pointed to the TV. "He wanted to get a better view of the football game." Cue the sad clown music. It's moments like this that I realize right about the time that I think we are doing something right and I start to get puffed up, God throws me a curveball to remind me we aren't all that and God is still the one in charge. (Cincinnati won, for the record.) Despite those guys not giving a shit about AfterHours and the very, very, very important, life-changing work we were doing, I was still glad they sat in. It was a win for me and my overinflated ego, and they got to come in contact with a very kind group of people.

So often we get concerned with what happens *after* our initial contact, whether our work has had the impact we want it to. That's God's gig. Our gig is just to make people feel welcome and to love them. This is really the job of us all. Find the maximum way to love people and be with them. That's it. It's our only job and our complete and total job description—no egos necessary.

Sometimes we'll be surprised. Recently I got a call on my phone from a number I didn't recognize. I let it go to voice mail, and a few minutes later I listened to it. It was from a server at one of our locations who said that while she was serving us the other night she was also listening. She wanted to know what days we were in the park and what time and if we could use another person. (Fred Craddock once wrote a book called *Overhearing the Gospel*. I get it now.)

I think this "everything depends on me" belief can cripple us. We get so serious. We need to lighten up, both in the church and out. The church seems to long ago have equated the sacred with the somber. I simply have not found that to be true. I know a number of homeless people who grasp this a lot better than those of us with a roof over our head. Our friends on the street have taught me this better than anyone. Few situations can be harder than living on the street, and yet they often find ways of making light of life. (I once asked a guy if he wanted Communion, and he looked at me and said, "Well, I'm sure as hell not here for the peanut butter!")

Having a sense of humor about life and at the same time having the humility to recognize that the world doesn't revolve around us are both useful tools in getting us through the hardest days.

Small, but Not Too Small

Throughout many of the conversations I have had with people who connect to God through activities outside the church, one overriding and often-mentioned description is that of humility. The activity, whether riding a horse, backpacking, or surfing, reminded the person how small they were in comparison with the rest of the world. The power of a majestic horse, the vastness of a mountain vista, or the enormity of a crushing wave each reminded the participants that they aren't all that.

For those of us who believe in God, that should make us feel small as well. The same God we can connect with on a personal level is the same God that created everyone and everything. Everything! Not just our planet but all planets. Not just our galaxy but every galaxy. The entire cosmos. The hugeness of the universe is enough to remind us that we aren't the center of that universe.

Here's the challenge, though. We shouldn't think too little of ourselves either. I believe one of the things that is at the center of all the problems in the world is a deep-seated sense of self-loathing.

In the Letter to the Romans (chapter 12, verse 3, for those of you playing along at home), Paul says this: "For by the grace given to me I say to everyone among you not to think of yourself more highly than you ought to think, but to think with sober judgment." While the temptation to insert a joke here around "sober judgment" is huge, the message is too great. Most of us struggle with thinking either too highly of ourselves or not highly enough. Sober judgment does not mean thinking poorly of yourself. It means thinking accurately of yourself—not too much, not too little. Someone once said that humility isn't thinking less of yourself—it's thinking of yourself less.

In the end, humility is about knowing your value and knowing what you are worth. It is knowing that you are special and unique and amazing. It is also knowing that you are no more special and unique and amazing than anyone else. It is not the "thinking you are great" part that is the problem. You are great! It is when you start to think that you are any greater than anyone else that it starts to go south. Most bravado is actually a cover for deep-seated insecurities. When we see someone who goes on and on about their own greatness, we can almost guarantee that underneath there is real pain.

We are called to love our neighbors as ourselves. That seems to mean that we have to love ourselves *first*. There has to be self-love for there to be love freely given. Too often we can give away so much that there is nothing left for ourselves. Can you say "burnout"?

For a lot of people, one of the ways to curb burnout is just to get out, to block off time that is for you and you alone. We have to find those ways to give back to ourselves and to be a little gentler with the person in the mirror. I have always had body issues, and I'm not the only one. At fifty-four, I have both wrinkles *and* zits. Part of me wants to scream, "There is no God!" but then I realize I am lucky to be taking a breath and that when anyone's biggest problems are that he has a blemish from eating too much chocolate or "laugh lines" from guffawing too much, then that person's life is pretty damn good. As my dad used to say, "Growing old isn't a lot of fun, but I'll take it over the alternative."

A pastor friend has said, "Even with all the advances in medical science, we still have a 100 percent mortality rate." We are blessed to be on this planet, and most of us reading this have been given many things. The fact that we can draw a breath is stunning! We are amazing! Now what are we going to do with all this amazingness? We cannot let even one moment get away from us. There is so much good to do, and we are just the amazing people to do it! With God's help we truly can change the world. I have seen it with my own two eyes. St. Augustine wrote, "Without God, we cannot. Without us, God will not." We matter to God! God wants to work with us and see us change the world. I believe it is this partnership that will ultimately fix and heal the planet. As a bonus, I think this will catapult us into joy and contentment, as I mentioned earlier. This joy and contentment will lead us to gratitude, which in return will create a desire to give back in an attitude of thanks. And here we see the good coming full circle. That doesn't suck.

Hustling for Worth

Too often we forget who we are and where we came from. Our essence is amazingness, and if we would just relax and stop trying so damn hard, we would remember that. It is usually in the trying so hard that we screw it up. I will be the first to admit I am not there yet. In fact, I have a long way to go. I still catch myself striving, still watch myself push and push and push. I'm not proud of that. That then creates self-loathing, which perpetuates the cycle. The hamster wheel of low self-esteem and irritating ego is not a pretty ride.

Never good enough. That is often the subtle message that plays in a lot of our heads. I think it is never more prevalent than at the beginning of the year. Resolutions are in essence an admission that we are not good enough. This often leads to what Brené Brown calls "hustling for our own worthiness"[1]—doing just a little bit more so that we can finally claim we are worthy.

I would love to say that this is a lesson *I* am going to teach *you*. I would love to say I have this mastered. The sad truth is that I still struggle with this every damn day. I have to remind myself constantly *why* I do this work, *why* I hustle, *why* I am doing more—because I want to be clear: there is nothing wrong with hustling. There is nothing wrong with being the best you can be. There is nothing wrong with trying to achieve goals. But behind all of it, we have to ask, "Why?" Why are we hustling, and being our best, and achieving goals? In a nutshell: Who is this for and why?

I have a friend I'll call Mark. Mark had a horrible childhood. His mother made no qualms about the fact that getting pregnant with him ruined her life and that he was worthless. He left home at sixteen.

He runs his own company now and makes a ton of money. He has all the trappings of success and can afford pretty much anything he wants. He is, by all accounts, very successful.

I asked him one time if he thought his mother's harsh words fueled his desire to succeed. "No doubt about it," he said. "I know that most everything I've done is to show her that I am not worthless and that I have succeeded in the past and will continue to succeed in the future."

His mom has been dead for over twenty years.

He is hustling to get the approval of someone who can never give it to him. And even if she were alive, she probably never would.

A number of us chase after our parents' approval. Some of us let that go years ago but then found someone else to fill in that gap: siblings, friends, colleagues, even strangers.

I have struggled with each of these. First it was my dad when I was growing up, then my brother, then Hollywood, then society. My latest struggle is fighting against my tendency to try and win the approval of my colleagues. Oddly, after much time with my therapist, I came to the realization that it wasn't my colleagues in general who were holding back their approval. It was a very specific group, whose "Well done" or "Nice job" or "That was awesome" I was desperate for. This group really isn't a group at all, but just a few people. They will never give that approval, and that's OK.

There is one whose approval we don't need to seek, one we don't have to "do better for," one we don't have to hustle for our worth. We can stop hustling for our worthiness from God.

When I pray with the guys on the street, I remind them that there is nothing they have done, are doing, or will do that will make God stop loving them. They are enough. Already. We are enough. Already. We can rest. While the world and our colleagues and spouses and friends and family might need us to be better, God loves us right here, right now. Not because *we* are awesome . . . but because *God* is awesome. That's just how God rolls.

This flies in the face of how a lot of us were brought up—that we had to "earn" God's favor, that all we had to do was pray enough, or go to church enough, or memorize the Bible enough, or be on enough committees, or volunteer enough. Once we hit that magic number, we would be worthy in God's eyes. Some of us even believe that it's our "right actions" and/or "right beliefs" that will one day "earn" our way into heaven.

This question of what we need to do to be good enough on a spiritual level has been screwing with people's minds for years. Even in the Bible, we see this issue being debated:

> What good is it, my brothers and sisters, if you say you have faith but do not have works? Can faith save you? If a brother or sister is naked and lacks daily food, and one of you says to them, "Go in peace; keep warm and eat your fill," and yet you do not supply their bodily needs, what is the good of that? So faith by itself, if it has no works, is dead. (James 2:14–17)

To be clear, these aren't instructions on how to get into heaven. There is no mention of that. What this passage is saying is that to just talk about what we believe really doesn't transform us. Transformation comes when we see our actions change how we live our life. As Peter Rollins says, "Authentic faith is expressed, not in the mere acceptance of a belief system, but in sacrificial, loving action."[2] It is how our beliefs function that matter.

That said, we have to be careful not to fall into the trap of believing we are "better than" anyone because of the work we choose to do. I don't think we serve to "win" anything from God or others. I think that can turn us toward worthiness: the more we do, the more worthy we are; the less we do, the less worthy we are. Danger! Danger!

Service is a way to simply live out gratitude. It is not done to "win" anything. It is done as a way of saying thank you. Thank you for letting me open my eyes today, for letting me breathe and get out of bed and have a roof over my head and food in my belly. Thank you for my friends and family, even the ones who drive me nuts. Thank you that I have work to do and that I get paid for it. Thank you that I live in this country, as messed up as it is. There is electricity and running water and roads that can get us from here to there.

Jim McKeever is one of the leaders at AfterHours here in Denver and is the other half of "the Jims" I mentioned earlier. Monday through Thursday, Jim leaves his job working for the city of Denver and walks over to Civic Center Park, where we hand out the lunches and the love. I asked Jim why he does this almost every single day he's at work, throughout year. He responded, "I try to live from a position of gratitude. I have no doubt that I can never 'earn' any brownie points with God, but I think I do have a responsibility to express my thankfulness for all I have been given, and the best way to do this is to share with those who have less. Whether it be money, food, time, or just a smile, I always have something to give, and in doing so, I have shared a bit of God with that person. Of course, being with those less fortunate also helps me to more fully appreciate how truly blessed I am, and even on my worst days, it reminds me that life is good." That is a solid theology.

Gratitude is a way of seeing the world in a way that you can't help but want to give back. It is putting on the glasses that show that most of us reading this have been blessed with time and money and privileges and abilities that many people in the world can only dream of. When we have been given so much and have taken the time to be *aware* of it, how can we not want to give back in one way or another? Gratitude is simply saying thanks.

What it is not is a constant hustle to earn our worthiness. We can get off the treadmill. We can stop running. We can stop the hustle. We are enough.

Believe it. And give back.

FOR HEATHENS' EYES ONLY

French 75

This drink is named after a French artillery cannon and will knock you on your ass. Proceed with caution.

Like the Sazerac and the Vieux Carre, the French 75 also was birthed in New Orleans. It's a pretty drink. Don't let it fool ya.

1/2 oz. lemon juice
1/2 oz. simple syrup (or 1 tsp. sugar)
2 oz. London dry gin or cognac
Champagne, chilled

Add the lemon juice and simple syrup to a shaker, and stir to combine. Add the gin and fill with ice. Shake, and strain into a Collins glass filled with cracked ice. Fill slowly with champagne.

Chapter Five

A Church That Doesn't Suck

THE SPIRITUALITY OF . . . PAINTING

It's not every day that one gets to interview someone who has worked on an Academy Award–nominated picture. Dena Petersen was one of the animators for Loving Vincent, *which was nominated for best animated film in 2018.*

Dena finds spirituality in a brush and paints and canvas. I asked her about what makes that activity sacred. "I often feel a connection to God through painting," she told me. "It isn't necessarily something that others might experience." (This is crucial: Just because the activities mentioned throughout this book provide a connection for the people being interviewed, that doesn't mean they will for every person out there—you know, just like church.) At an earlier time in life, painting helped Dena connect to "a peace and joy that I had not felt before." After taking a break from painting to work in psychology and raise three kids, she returned to painting and found that sense of peace again. "It felt more like the presence of God in my life," she said.

Painting has allowed Dena to express herself without judgment or self-consciousness. She shared with me a quote by Vincent van Gogh: "If you hear a voice within you saying, 'You are not a painter,' then by all means paint, boy, and that voice will be silenced, but only by working." There is power in the doing.

"It's really hard work," she told me. "Painting has sometimes been idealized or romanticized." But her love of the craft overcomes the hard work involved.

Dena was quick to say that she sometimes feels the act of painting to be selfish, but I couldn't disagree more. To give people the gift of connecting with their feelings? What a beautiful gift to give. She did acknowledge, "If my passion and emotion can touch someone else, maybe it's of value." Never underestimate the value of putting more beauty and joy into the world. That is a gift that is tailor-made to be given away.

Dena didn't bring home the Oscar that night in March for Loving Vincent. *I still think it's safe to say, "And the winner is . . ."*

If there's one story that sums up AfterHours in a nutshell, it's this one: Heather has been coming to AfterHours for a couple of years now. She is a good old-fashioned southern girl with a love of leopard prints and roller derby. In fact, she started a roller derby league back in her home state of Alabama. She is smart and funny and has a deep love of Jesus. She has also been screwed over a time or two by organized religion and the world in general.

That is a common theme at AfterHours: people who have been bent over by church and religion. Amazingly, most of these folks have the wisdom to know it wasn't God that was leading the charge as much as it was flawed people—flawed people who happen to go to church. The folks who come to AfterHours resemble the folks who go to my friend Trey Hall's church, Urban Village in

Chicago. When someone asks Trey who goes to Urban Village, he says, "The burned and the bored." That pretty well describes the people at AfterHours as well. We are like the Island of Misfit Toys, and our Heather doll might not work exactly right and might be a little broken but will love you back with a vengeance, along with a grace not often found in the pews, or even the world for that matter. She is a free spirit that will not be caged, and she brings wisdom and vulnerability to our community. She is like our Maya Angelou with platform heels and a dirty mouth. She discovered AfterHours through Steve, another of our regulars, who saw our AfterHours ad while he was trying to find good prices for weed in Denver's local free paper.

One day about a year or two back, Heather came up to me very excited. "Guess what! I'm in a burlesque workshop, and for our final we get to do a routine for a show we are doing for the public, and you have to come!" I missed very few classes in seminary, but I'm pretty sure this was never covered. She was so pumped up, and I had no desire to puncture that excitement. Having said that, I was almost positive that it's not good protocol to watch any of your congregants take their clothes off on any stage, let alone one where there might be a pole present. She told me that the class was one of the most powerful things she had ever done, that it gave her newfound confidence about herself and her body, and that when she was on stage she felt empowered and strong and proud of who she was. So now what? Before I could answer, Heather was off notifying others about the show and telling them to hold the date.

In moments like these I turn to some of my smart, funny, way-wiser-than-I female clergy colleagues and ask them what I should do.

One of these colleagues—another Heather, oddly enough—is whip smart and as quick-witted as they come. After I told her the story and shared with her my dilemma, she quickly responded, "You mean you are wondering what you should do when a woman in your congregation asks you to support her in something that makes her feel strong, empowered, and confident? You are trying to figure out whether or not you should support her?"

Well, when you put it that way . . .

Rev. Heather advised getting other AfterHours people to go, bringing my wife, Laura, along, and supporting Burlesque Heather in this new thing that has given her life. That became the plan. As fate would have it, however, I ended up having to be out of town and wasn't there for the show—awkwardness averted. But that's not the end of the story.

A bunch of AfterHours people did end up going to the show. We AfterHours folks can, on occasion, be a bit of a rowdy bunch, and that night proved to be no exception. According to the reports I received, when Heather got on stage, our people started hooting and hollering. As she finished her routine three-and-a-half minutes later, the AfterHours folks went berserk. When Heather got off stage, her instructor, a lifelong dancer who "had seen it all," was right there waiting for her. She couldn't believe the ruckus the AfterHours folks were making. She turned to Heather and said, "My God, that's awesome. All those people came for you. Who are they? How do you know them?" Heather just looked at her, smiled a big, shit-eating grin, and said, "That's my church!"

That's the kind of thing that happens at AfterHours. We collect people who like to have a good time, who might curse too much, who might be hungover more than sometimes, who ride motorcycles too fast, who might fall in love too easily on a Friday night, and who might, just might, smoke a little bit of weed. Relax, it's Colorado. (I am relatively sure Denver is one of the only places in the country where you can see homeless people standing outside of dispensaries and hear them say to people leaving the store, "Hey man, can you spare a little cannabis?" But I digress.)

There is a huge possibility that the lives of people at AfterHours are not going exactly right. We are gay and straight and coupled and uncoupled, black and white and trans and everything along the spectrum. We know we don't get it right all the time—hell, maybe even most of the time. But in the end we have two things going for us: a love of people and a love of God. We are a community that comes together to hear each other's woes and to rejoice and maybe do a shot when someone lands a new job. We have love at the core.

Recently at AfterHours we talked about getting to choose the frame we want to live in. We choose the narrative. We can focus on the joy and light and good, or we can focus on the darkness. Afterward, when we did Communion, people hugged Dottie and me as we gave them the bread and juice. I had never been hugged during Communion before. I love my church.

As different as we all are on the surface, underneath the epidermis, we still have one thing in common. When seven o'clock on a Monday night rolls around, we all stop what we are doing, throw on some plastic gloves, scoop out some peanut butter, and come together to feed a stranger. We have done this from the very start, even when we were still just a ministry out of St. Andrew and had not even started doing services in bars. Serving the poor has been mission critical since day one. (One of my clergy friends sent me a meme after a conversation we had about this very thing. On it there was only one sentence. "First came the poor . . . then came the pour." Amen.)

The Spirituality of a Good Bar

As William Blake alluded to in his poem "The Little Vagabond" in 1789, "A good local pub has much in common with a church, except that a pub is warmer, and there's more conversation."

I think Billy B. had it right. Churches and pubs have more in common than most people would see at first blush. Of course, people push back on this right off the bat because of the booze. I think that's a mistake.

Sociologist Ray Oldenberg first coined the term "third place" in 1989 in his book *The Good Great Place*. It isn't home. It isn't work. It is your "third place"—a place to hang out, a place to have great discussions and debates, a place where all are equal and there is community thick as honey.

The Good Great Place was instrumental in the creation of AfterHours. I devoured that book. Oldenberg visited bistros in France, beer gardens in Germany, pubs in England and Ireland. He spent a huge amount of time in diners, barbershops, and beauty parlors in the United States. Booze is not a requirement of being a third place. Because Oldenberg was a sociologist, he measured everything—including, if the place served alcohol, the number of drinks people had and at what pace. He discovered that alcohol might correlate to deeming a location a third place, but it wasn't a cause of that.

What became evident was that community was central. There was a sense, as the *Cheers* theme song says, that it was a place where everyone knows your name.

Thin Man is a third place for me. It is a bar in Denver that doesn't open until 3 p.m., so I don't get in as often as I would like (I am usually trying to beat traffic back to my end of town by three), but when I do walk in, Tyron always greets me warmly, remembers my drink, and always plays the best music. (Today it's the James Brown channel on Pandora.)

Thin Man is one of the most popular bars in Denver, but since I'm there when it opens, it's usually dead. That's fine. The spirituality of a bar is not dictated by the number of customers it has. It has to do with "the bones" of the place. With only fourteen seats at the bar, six four-tops and five two-top tallboy tables, there are fewer than fifty seats in the whole joint. But it is soaked in soul. One entire wall is covered with religious icons (including a black-velvet picture of Jesus hovering over an eighteen-wheeler), a result of the bar owner's claim to be "a fallen Eastern Orthodox."

It is not any one thing that gives a bar its spirituality. It is more than the sum of its parts. It's an ethos, a feeling. It's how the place makes you feel when you walk in. It's how its people make you feel.

I am blessed to have access to a number of these places in Denver: Euclid Hall, Don's Mixed Drinks, the Irish Rover, El Chapultepec, Nallen's, White Chocolate Grill, Seven Grand. I have had some of my deepest and most spiritual conversations in these joints with both strangers and old friends alike. Many times I have no idea what these people do, where they are from, or even what their last names are. Some I have seen dozens of times. Some

I will never see again. That doesn't matter. There is a respect and connection that come through these places and their people.

As William Blake would say, the place is just warm. And the conversation is always plentiful.

If you find a church that feels like that—awesome. We should sing it from the rooftops, take out full-page ads, and tell the world. Hopefully other people will dig it too. But don't go because you fear hell. God functions out of love, never fear. Fear is a lousy motivator in the long run. It works great in the short term, but fear can never hold. Only love can bring you in and keep you. And don't go out of guilt. God sees through all that crap anyway. Do we really think we are pulling anything over on God? And if we *haven't* been going but feel guilty, we need to stop that too. Guilt sucks, and there are probably a billion other things we should feel guilty about. We shouldn't let church be one of them.

We should come together not because we are scared of hell. We should come together not because of guilt. We should come together to be a community that loves and cares for each other. A community that wants to take that love and care and spread that shit out in the world thick like peanut butter!

Few things feel as good as sharing good news and watching the joy in other people's eyes at hearing it. On the flip side of that same coin, I truly believe that grief is divided when it is shared with others. It's not that misery loves company; it's that misery *needs* company. I believe that it is when we come together to share in another's pain we are most accurately living like Christ. Jesus *never* ran away from pain—he ran toward it. He knew that when we share our pain, it lessens, and it is there that the Holy

Spirit, whatever *that* is, can enter in and be part of the healing. Each of us is a roadway that helps the Holy Spirit get to where it needs to go. Nothing fixes others *and* us more than caring for someone. This is what a beloved community looks like.

No, it's not always easy, but it is holy.

The other day, a young woman showed up in the park. We were almost done, and we probably had about a half-dozen lunches left. It was pretty clear by the way she was rocking and walking in circles and almost nodding off while standing up that she was rollin' pretty good. She never even really got in line, so I just kind of shouted at her from about ten feet away, "Hey there, do you want something to eat?"

She never really even looked up, but she did start to walk over to me. I hadn't seen her before, and trust is a hard thing to gain on the street, so I wasn't surprised at her being so hesitant.

She got to where I was standing at the Communion table, and before I could offer her one of our last sack lunches, she grabbed half the loaf of Communion bread, dunked it halfway deep into the grape juice, pulled it out, and stuck it in her mouth. Then she turned and walked away.

And just like that, we were done with Communion for the day.

As a former Catholic, my head almost exploded. I had a million emotions in a matter of seconds. I didn't view it as a sin or even necessarily "wrong." It was just the idea that she was eating the "heavenly host" like chips and salsa just didn't sit right with me.

The more I thought about it, though, the more I realized that what I had witnessed was probably pretty close to the "Last Supper" that inspired the Communion ritual. When Jesus first broke bread, it was a blessing and then a celebration of a meal with his friends. I am guessing that Jesus would have no problem with the woman's "grab and dunk" approach.

The first rule of serving the poor: We take people where they are at. We don't require them to be a certain way to receive God's love and grace. It took a junkie on a cold January afternoon on the streets of Denver to remind me. Thanks be to God.

So often the church and organized religion put a bunch of requirements in front of people before they can be part of the community. The language used is "commitment." You have to be committed. You have to be "intentional." You have to want it.

In general, I don't struggle with those ideas. I think you have to be committed to your family, your diet, your workout, your career. Things don't just fall from the sky. Rarely is anything free.

Except grace. Grace *does* fall from the sky. Jesus' whole work while he was here was to remind people that they were loved and that they were worthy right where they were. God would love them right there, regardless of their tithe, their Sunday attendance, or the number of times they taught Sunday school. Giving to the building campaign wasn't a prerequisite for God's love. Yet the church's requirements always seem to be higher than Jesus' own.

I don't know what a lot of churches would do if someone grabbed the Communion bread and dunked it in the sacramental wine. Jesus himself probably would have anticipated what she was going to do, torn the huge piece in two, and dunked them both—one for her, one for him.

No one should eat alone.

Put More Love into the World—and Relax

It is often those moments in community when "study" is over and people have had a few drinks that people's guards come down. They leave the bullshit and the things they are "supposed to say" behind and go to another level. You start to realize at times like these that it doesn't have to be complicated. You realize the power of actions over words, kindness over cleverness, and simplicity over complex doctrine. You really start to see the power of feeling safe in a community of people you love and who simply won't judge you, a community of people who have taken the time to know you.

It was a group of friends like this who best put my theology into words based on an amalgam of Facebook posts and conversations over a couple of long lunches and possibly a few cocktails:

1. There is nothing you can do to make God love you more.
2. There is nothing you can do to make God love you less.
3. Don't be a dick.

In short, that's my theology. Relax and take a breath; it's going to be fine. We have an amazing, stunning, beautiful world crammed with good. Enjoy it. I know too many people who confuse being a "good Christian" with connecting to God. Don't do that. There is a difference between being a good Christian and trying to connect to God. Being a good Christian means trying to live like Jesus, which requires service and sacrifice. Again, it's simple, just not easy.

Be willing to expand your idea of what service in the

world looks like, especially if you have a unique gift to share. I know sometimes you want to sleep in. Me too. Go ahead. That's fine. But sometimes, we need to get our lazy asses out of bed and help a fellow human being. Make someone else's life a little easier, shovel a walk, feed a homeless dude, leave a little bit extra for a tip—hell, hold a door open for somebody. In short, put more love in the world. If nothing else, you'll feel better. And yeah, if that's a little selfish, so be it. Consider it a win/win and get on with it.

Lighten up on yourself. You are doing the best you can at this moment. You are amazing, and God has a kickass plan for your life—a life that includes love and joy and happiness and a ton of the good stuff. But you can *start* with loving yourself. Make that happen. Drop everything else and invest in yourself first—not your kids, not your spouse, not your work or your siblings or your friends or the dude or dudette you are sleeping with. You. Because if you give to everyone else first and save what's left over for you, you will lose. You might not admit it or honestly even know it, but that's the kind of crap that backs up on you. Do whatever work you have to do to make yourself ass-kicking great. Remember, you are a rock that God threw in the lake of life. There are ripples that come out from you. The bigger and better the rock that is you, the bigger and better the ripples will be. Do your damnedest to create tidal waves.

Find people to help you on this journey, because it is hard as hell to do alone. We are wired for community. I think we thrive in the presence of others. To be clear, I am not talking about being around people just to be around people. That blows. Small talk and mindless chit-chat are a pain in the ass, and I know very few people who like it, even extroverts.

I am talking about community—real community, a group of people you can cry with and who will hold you while you sob or laugh with you until you pee. Find these people. Treasure these people. Do not let these people go. Find the tribe that will cheer you during the good, hug you during the bad, and let you know when you are an ass when you need it.

In short, these people will help you be the best you can be—maybe not a saint, but something damn near close.

FOR HEATHENS' EYES ONLY

Sazerac

1 sugar cube
1 dash Angostura bitters
2 dashes Peychaud's bitters
2 oz. rye (the original recipe called for cognac)
A few drops of absinthe
A strip of lemon peel

Throw an old-fashioned glass in the freezer. (Better yet, keep a couple in there at all times.) In a second old-fashioned glass, muddle the sugar cube with the Angostura and the Peychaud's bitters.

Add ice and the rye. Stir.

Pull the first old-fashioned glass out of the freezer. (I usually rinse my glass with some water prior to putting it in so that it gets a nice frost on it.) Put a few drops of absinthe in this glass, and turn it so the absinthe coats the inside of the glass. Discard any that's not on the walls of the glass.

Strain the glass with the rye in it into the chilled glass you took out of the freezer.

Cut a strip of lemon peel and squeeze it over the drink. Some say discard the lemon peel so that the drink has no garnish at all. I say put it in. We aren't heathens.

On second thought, leave it out.

Notes

Introduction

1. Rice University's Baker Institute Speech, October 26, 1999.

Chapter 1. Things God Does (and Doesn't) Care About

1. "Sonic Evolution with the Use of Tool," *Boston Globe*, November 15, 1996.

2. Sallie McFague, *Blessed Are the Consumers: Climate Change and the Practice of Restraint* (Minneapolis: Fortress Press: 2013), 9, 22.

Chapter 2. Do Justice: Service and Beyond

1. "How Many People Are Hungry in the World?," Hunger Notes, December 28, 2016, https://www.worldhunger.org/hunger-quiz/how-many-people-are-hungry-in-the-world.

2. Stephanie Watson, "Volunteering May Be Good for Your Body and Mind," Harvard Health Publishing, June 26, 2013, https://www.health.harvard.edu/blog/volunteering-may-be-good-for-body-and-mind-201306266428.

3. Anna Bernasek, "Volunteering in America Is on the Decline," *Newsweek*, September 23, 2014, https://www.newsweek.com/2014/10/03/volunteering-america-decline-272675.html.

4. Martin Luther King Jr., "The Drum Major Instinct" (sermon, Ebenezer Baptist Church, Atlanta, GA, February 4, 1968).

Chapter 3. Love Kindness: Don't Be an Asshat

1. Richard Rohr, *Things Hidden: Scripture as Spirituality* (London: SPCK Publishing, 2016), 76, 77.

2. Wes Angelozzi, Timeline photo, November 12, 2015, retrieved from http://m.facebook.com/wesangelozzi1111/photos.a.1675999436 008800/1676214112653999/?type=3&source=54.

3. Frederick Buechner, *Wishful Thinking: A Theological ABC* (San Francisco: Harper One, 1993), 118, 119.

Chapter 4. Walk Humbly, with Your Head Held High

1. Brené Brown, *The Gifts of Imperfection: Let Go of Who You Think You're Supposed to Be and Embrace Who You Are* (Center City, MN: Hazelden Publishing, 2010), 23.

2. Peter Rollins, *The Orthodox Heretic and Other Impossible Tales* (Brewster, MA: Paraclete Press, 2009), 8.